Gillian

111 Places
in Fife
That You
Shouldn't Miss

111

emons:

©Bibliographical information of the Deutsche Nationalbibliothek
The Deutsche Nationalbibliothek lists this publication
in the Deutsche Nationalbibliografie; detailed bibliographical data
are available on the internet at http://dnb.d-nb.de.

© Emons Verlag GmbH
All rights reserved
All photographs by Gillian Tait
© Cover icon: shutterstock.com/Patricia Chumillas
Layout: Editorial Design & Artdirection, Conny Laue, Bochum,
based on a design by Lübbeke | Naumann | Thoben
Maps: altancicek.design, www.altancicek.de
Basic cartographical information from Openstreetmap,
© OpenStreetMap-Mitwirkende, OdbL
Editing: Ros Horton
Printing and binding: Grafisches Centrum Cuno, Calbe
Printed in Germany 2022
ISBN 978-3-7408-1740-4
Revised third edition, October 2022

Guidebooks for Locals & Experienced Travellers
Join us in uncovering new places around the world at
www.111places.com

Foreword

There are a host of apt quotations that perfectly describe diverse aspects of this fascinating little Kingdom, and a select few are to be found within these pages. But the old saying that best sums up my personal experience of putting this book together is 'Bid farewell to Scotland, and cross to Fife'. The wedge-shaped peninsula that I've always thought of as a Scottie dog nosing the North Sea has such a distinctive quality that it can feel like another country.

Although I spent many weeks as a temporary resident of towns including Cupar, Burntisland, Kirkcaldy and Strathkinness, much of the research and photography for this book was done on day trips from my home in Edinburgh. And it's no exaggeration to say that every time I crossed the Forth to Fife, by train, bus or car, I felt a keen sense of adventure akin to the excitement of going abroad. It all added up to a true voyage of discovery, involving a great deal of hugely enjoyable travel, exploring territory both familiar and previously unknown to me.

The overwhelming majority of the places in this guide are easily accessible by public transport, and that's how I chose to get to nearly all of them myself. With the exception of some rush-hour rail services (best avoided) I found both trains and buses to be remarkably punctual and reliable as well as, in many cases, woefully under-occupied – I was often the sole passenger on rural minibus routes.

I'm not sure who came up with the slogan 'Variety is the spice of Fife', but it's a neat summation of the exceptional range of delights that the Kingdom has to offer. I do hope that my texts and photos succeed in conveying my enormous enthusiasm for every one of these 111 unique places – and, equally, their accompanying tips.

Gillian Tait

111 Places

1 Aberdour Castle

Pigeons in the beehive and rabbits in the pillows

Exploring Scottish castles is a bit of a hit-and-miss affair: it can mean anything from strolling round the palatial interior and extensive grounds of a desirable country residence to stumbling over the dismal remains of some battered old bulwark. Aberdour Castle is somewhere in between: unmodernised since its owners left in the 1720s after a fire, it offers easily digestible tastes of both extremes, along with intriguing insights into the changing aspirations of the Scottish élite over the five-century span of its occupancy.

The story begins with the Anglo-Norman baron Alan de Mortimer, who acquired Aberdour in the early 12th century; enough remains of his sturdy keep to show the sophistication of his Frenchified ways. A couple of centuries later the estate passed to the ambitious Douglas family, who gradually enlarged the building into a classic tower house. In the 1560s this was developed into a Renaissance mansion after Aberdour came into the hands of its most notorious resident, James Douglas, fourth Earl of Morton. A Machiavellian politician, Morton was the power behind the throne of Mary, Queen of Scots, and became regent of Scotland after forcing her abdication.

In 1567, the Privy Council met at his fashionable residence, where they would certainly have admired its corridors (a novelty) as well as the fine terraced grounds. These functioned not only as pleasure gardens but as a sort of living larder, featuring a formidable beehive-shaped dovecot, with nesting boxes for 600 pigeons, and 'pillow mounds' – oblong sand heaps where unsuspecting rabbits made their warrens. The estate grew further in grandeur under the 8th Earl, who added the lavishly furnished east range – the ghost of a jolly painted ceiling survives – and maintained a large walled garden burgeoning with fruit and vegetables, native and exotic. The nobility always made sure they ate well. Today, humbler visitors may share in the autumn bounty of the apple orchard, for a nominal charge.

Address Aberdour, KY3 0SL, +44 (0)1383 860519, www.historicenvironment.scot | Getting there Train to Aberdour; the castle is right next to the railway station, which also has a large, free car park | Hours Apr–Sept, daily 9.30 am–5.30 pm, Oct–Mar, Sat–Wed 10 am–4 pm | Tip Be sure not to miss the ancient St Fillan's Kirk, a peaceful place closely connected to the eventful history of the castle, accessed from a gate in the walled garden. Still a working church, it has a beautifully simple Romanesque nave and chancel dating from c1140.

2 The *Orontes* Ceiling

First-class glass that sailed down under

Known to the Victorians as the jewel of the Fife Riviera, Aberdour became a popular holiday destination thanks to the paddle steamers that once plied the Firth of Forth, and the elegantly spired Woodside Hotel, built in 1873 to cater to the better class of tripper, still dominates the heart of the town. In the late 1920s the hotel's west wing was given a fashionable palm-court atmosphere by the installation of a magnificent stained-glass vault, supported on elaborately carved woodwork. A close inspection of this carving reveals the surprising sight of fauna not normally spotted in Fife – a kangaroo and an emu, proudly flanking an emblematic shield. This offers a clue to the ceiling's far-flung history: for the first 24 years of its life it was the centrepiece of the first-class dining saloon on an ocean liner that travelled between London and Australia.

That ship was the RMS *Orontes*, run by the Orient Line, all of whose vessels had names beginning with O. (The original Orontes is a river in the Levant.) Built in 1902 at the Clydeside Fairfield yard, to carry 1,000 passengers and a cargo of mail to Melbourne and Sydney, she later made voyages to Africa and America, and also spent time as a troopship during World War I. But by the 1920s she was no longer up to the standard required of passenger liners, and in 1926 she was scrapped at Ward's yard in Inverkeithing, just down the coast from Aberdour. Shipbreakers were only interested in metal parts, and were happy to part with the furnishings – though salvaging an entire glazed ceiling for the enterprising owner of the Woodside must have been quite a feat. The exquisite stained glass is the work of the unjustly forgotten Oscar Paterson, a key exponent of the Glasgow Style whose studio was one of the most acclaimed and influential in the UK in the decades around 1900, supplying churches and grand residences throughout Britain, Europe and the Empire as well as several liners, including the ill-fated *Lusitania*.

Address Woodside Hotel, 78 High Street, Aberdour, KY3 0SW, +44 (0)1383 860328, woodsidehotelaberdour.co.uk | Getting there Train to Aberdour | Hours The ceiling is in the Clipper Room. The hotel is now an exclusive use venue, for parties of up to 24 guests. See website for details. | Tip The Woodside is also a venue for intimate live music gigs, featuring artists such as China Crisis, Mari Wilson and Rab Noakes. Pre-gig meal and overnight stay options are available. If you prefer quieter recreation, take a walk down to the secluded Black Sands beach.

3_ The Lime Kilns

The miraculous powder that came from the stones

Anyone who chances on Charlestown's waterfront by fluke or egregious satnav blunder might wonder if they've discovered a lost outpost of the Roman Empire: the imposing ranks of masonry arches built into the cliffside appear almost like a fragment of an ancient amphitheatre. But in fact they date from the beginning of the industrial era, and their purpose was far from recreational.

Now silent, derelict and firmly gated, these vaulted chambers once housed massive stone furnaces that glowed day and night as hosts of workers toiled to produce one of the most important commodities of the 18th and 19th centuries: lime. Their construction began in the revolutionary 1760s when the local landowner, Charles Bruce, 5th Earl of Elgin, resolved to maximise the potential of his estate's rich seams of limestone – a pale grey rock made from the fossilised shells of ancient sea creatures – and of coal. A good supply of the latter was essential for the transformation of the former into the valuable and highly versatile powder.

Lime had been prized for thousands of years for its quasi-mystical properties and myriad applications, not only in building but in farming, iron- and glass-making and medicine. Its manufacture on an industrial scale at Charlestown was hugely significant for the construction trade (not least in the emerging New Town of Edinburgh) and, though it may seem paradoxical for such a grimy business, equally crucial in fuelling a local green revolution, since its widespread use as a fertiliser dramatically improved the productivity of Fife's arable land. The state-of-the-art Charlestown limeworks soon became one of the largest complexes of its kind in the whole of the UK, with a harbour built expressly to allow ships to get close to the kilns, and a horse-drawn tramway linking them to the quarry. By 1837 the plant employed over 200 men. Quarrying ceased a century later, though the kilns continued in operation until as late as 1956.

Address East Harbour Road, Charlestown, KY11 3EA | **Getting there** Bus 6 to Charlestown (Saltpans) | **Hours** Viewable from the outside only | **Tip** The model village of Charlestown, just north of the harbour, was begun in 1761 to house workers. Its core streets are laid out in the form of the letters C and E, for Charles Elgin. The Scottish Lime Centre, at 2 Rocks Road, KY11 3EN, offers advice and training courses at all levels in traditional building skills. It has an illuminating exhibition on the subject of lime (Mon–Fri 8.30am–4.30pm).

4 _ Jim Baxter

The man who played keepy-uppy at Wembley

One of the most iconic games in Scottish football history was the national team's 3−2 victory at Wembley against reigning world champions England, on 15 April, 1967. It's a match that's remembered not just for the inventive playing of the whole Scotland squad, but for a particularly audacious display of skill by midfielder extraordinaire Jim Baxter. Keen to show up the England team's unimaginative play and taunt the 'Auld Enemy', Baxter spent crucial moments cheekily playing keepy-uppy – juggling the ball between his instep, knees and forehead – to the consternation of his opponents and delectation of the fans.

Such a show of nonchalant superiority was typical of the Fifer known fondly as Slim Jim. Arguably Scotland's greatest ever footballer, Baxter was a unique talent and a law unto himself who remains something of a folk hero to this day. Signed by Kirkcaldy's Raith Rovers at age 17, he progressed after three years to Glasgow Rangers, where he would eventually notch up 254 games as their number 6. He was a leading member of the international team from 1961 to 1967, gaining 34 caps in all for Scotland. At the same time his hedonistic off-pitch lifestyle became legendary, and it took its toll. He retired from football in 1970 at the age of 31 and soon went into a sad decline, characterised by two liver transplants, heavy gambling debts and divorce, before dying in 2001 at the age of 61.

His ashes were buried at Ibrox, home of Rangers F.C., but in 2003 his home village, Hill of Beath, unveiled a life-sized bronze by Andy Scott that immortalises the star in his prime, stroking the ball with his amazingly adept left foot, which he called 'the glove'. It was inaugurated with a speech by Gordon Brown, then Chancellor of the Exchequer, a long-time Baxter fan who helped raise funds for the statue by auctioning a replica of the famous budget briefcase. Fans still leave warm tributes beside the statue.

Address Ex-Service Memorial Club, Main Street, Hill of Beath, KY4 8DP | Getting there On B 917 at south-west edge of Cowdenbeath; bus 19/A/B/D, 33/A, X27, X54 or X59A to Hill of Beath (Concrete Works) | Tip Another Fife-born sporting hero of Baxter's generation was racing driver Jim Clark, one of the greatest ever stars of Formula One, who was killed in a crash in Germany in 1968. He is commemorated at his birthplace of Kilmany in a bronze statue by David Annand, unveiled in 1997 (KY15 4PT, just south of A 92).

5__ The Wee Miner Boy
Brightening up a grimy heritage

Cowdenbeath was built on coal. When the rich seams of the region were discovered in 1844, the settlement consisted of little more than a few farms and a coaching inn (where Queen Victoria had stopped off two years earlier, on her first trip to Scotland). Within a few decades it had become the centre of Britain's largest mining enterprise, the Fife Coal Company, and a veritable boom town: by 1914 its population had grown to 25,000, earning it the nickname 'The Chicago of Fife'. But in the 1930s the industry began an inexorable decline, and by the 1960s most of the deep pits that had been at the heart of the local economy were gone, and with them the proud cultural heritage and traditions of the miners.

Until recently, Cowdenbeath's most obvious reminder of this lost way of life was the mining subsidence for which the town was long notorious – apparent even in the High Street, where the once level roadway now has a pronounced dip. But since 2017 this same street has boasted a much more welcome memorial, in the form of a huge gable-end painting commissioned by the Community Council as part of a town centre improvement scheme. Officially called the Mining Heritage Mural, it's more familiarly known to artist Kerry Wilson as the Wee Miner Boy – despite being the biggest painting in Fife.

It was Kerry's first work on such a scale, though she had a variety of previous experience as a street artist, with a portfolio including the witty *Maci-Selfie,* which transformed a Glenrothes underpass into a giant mobile phone, and an acclaimed project to decorate the shutters of Cowdenbeath shops, carried out with the help of pupils from Beath High School. The mural is a positive image for a new generation now at more than one remove from the tough and grimy past of their community. It's a far cry from the harsh reality of lives spent 'howkin' awa neath a mountain o' stane' (in the words of pitman-poet Joe Corrie), but a warm tribute to them nonetheless.

Address Brunton Square, 353 High Street, Cowdenbeath, KY4 9QJ | **Getting there** Train to Cowdenbeath; bus X27, X54 or X59A to Broad Street (the Fountain) | **Tip** The nearby town of Lochgelly has a striking statue of a miner 'cracked and fractured like a coal seam', in the words of its sculptor, David Annand. Unveiled in 2008 as part of the town centre redevelopment, the sculpture is in the town square at the end of Main Street, near the former Miners' Institute.

6 Culross Palace

The glowing rewards of the Egyptian wheel

Seen from above, Culross might almost be a toy town, with its huddles of pristine red-roofed cottages flanking two big yellow dolls' houses. It's said that many tourists who walk the quiet cobbled wynds that doubled as the fictional Highland community of Cranesmuir in the *Outlander* series assume that it was built as a film set; even the electricity substation is hidden within a characterful old house. But the true history of this captivating little burgh (pronounced 'KOOriss') is much more surprising: it was in fact Scotland's earliest industrial town, an innovative centre for coal mining and its companion trades of salt making and iron working. This was thanks to the vision of merchant and engineer George Bruce, whose revolutionary Moat Pit, sunk around 1590, exploited a coal seam that ran under the River Forth, with a shaft extending 40 feet down from an artificial island offshore. The problem of drainage was solved by an ingenious mechanism known as the Egyptian wheel, a circulating chain of 36 buckets driven by three horses. But operations ceased when Bruce died in 1625, shortly after the pit was flooded by a storm. Culross then fell into a gradual decline, with the townscape of its 17th-century heyday preserved by its subsequent poverty.

Bruce's splendid 'Palace' was built from 1597 to 1611, close to the waterfront and his business ventures. It was derelict but largely unaltered when, in 1932, it was bought for just £700 by the nascent National Trust for Scotland, who then began a programme of restoration, in tandem with their work on the 'little houses' (see ch. 109). The exterior now glows with a traditional limewash, pigmented with copperas, while the warm, wood-panelled rooms have been furnished to give a highly evocative taste of the prosperous merchant's life; original features include a remarkable ceiling painted with allegorical scenes. At the rear is a thriving kitchen garden recreated in 17th-century style, complete with a brood of delightful Scots Dumpy hens.

Address West Green, Culross, KY12 8JH, +44 (0)1383 880359, www.nts.org | Getting there Bus 8/8B or 28 to Culross Palace | Hours Daily, Apr–Sept 10am–5pm, Oct 10am–4pm | Tip Opposite the Palace is a monument to controversial naval hero Thomas Cochrane, who helped the countries of Chile, Peru, Brazil and Greece gain independence. Follow the trail in the guidebook on sale at the Townhouse to see charming buildings such as the Study, with its quirky Outlook Tower – and don't miss Bruce's magnificently sculpted tomb in Culross Abbey.

7 __ Braefoot Point

Panoramas, pillboxes and petrochemicals

The Firth of Forth housed the most important naval base in the British Empire during World War I. In 1915, a battery was constructed at Braefoot Point that played a key role in its protection, with two 9.2-inch guns manned around the clock as an element in the second of three defence lines across the estuary, extending via Inchcolm to Cramond on the southern shore. The headland must have made a fine vantage point on 21 November, 1918, when, 10 days after the Armistice, some 440 warships – the largest armada in history – gathered in the waterway for the most extraordinary naval pageant ever staged, the surrender of Germany's mighty fleet.

A pleasant woodland now covers the site, shielding the silent relics among sycamores and banks of springtime bluebells. The military complex, bricked-up and graffitied but well preserved, includes gun emplacements, observation posts and barracks as well as part of the rail tracks linking the guns to the magazines. A path descends through gorse bushes to the shore, where the battery pier offers magnificent views upstream to the Forth Bridge and its two elegant companions. On the rocks nearby is a sign of renewed operations on the site during World War II: a hexagonal 'pillbox', one of thousands of deceptively cute little slit-eyed blockhouses built to guard Britain's coast. (The name alludes to postal pillar boxes, not medicine.)

The woodland also serves to obscure much of a vast monument of our own times: the Braefoot Bay marine terminal, whose twin-spur jetty suddenly looms into view to the east, extending into the waters of the eerily named Mortimer's Deep. Supertankers of up to 300,000 tons berth here to be loaded with liquefied petroleum gas, piped from the Mossmorran plant, over four miles away, where natural gas from the North Sea is processed. As you explore the woods, the continuous background hum of the pipelines is clearly audible, an awesome but disquieting reminder of our fossil-fuel-hungry age.

Address Braefoot Point, Dalgety Bay, KY11 9YS | Getting there Bus 7 or X58 to Moray Way North (Pentland Rise), walk east to St Colme Drive and join the Fife Coastal Path, continue until the right turn signposted to Braefoot Woods | Tip The well-preserved ruin of St Bridget's Kirk stands on a secluded site by the shore, just off the coastal path, at the end of Four Lums Road. The former parish church dates from 1170; features include a post-Reformation laird's loft, some beautiful 17th-century grave monuments and a watchtower built to deter body-snatchers.

8 Donibristle

In search of Lady Mondegreen

Scotland's first privately built new town, Dalgety Bay, owes its genesis in the early 1960s to the construction of the Forth Road Bridge and the resulting fast link for commuters to Edinburgh. In the era prior to the appearance of the first executive homes, the sprawling site now covered by 'the Bay' had a wide variety of occupants, from the fisherfolk of the lost ancient village of Dalgety to the World War I airmen at Donibristle aerodrome. But its best-known native son was undoubtedly the dashing young James Stewart, Earl of Moray, who was hacked to death on the Donibristle shore as his manor was burned to the ground by his arch-enemy the Earl of Huntly, on 7 February, 1592. The crime was widely condemned, and a sympathetic ballad soon gained currency that immortalised him for all time as 'The Bonny Earl o' Moray'.

Its anonymous author could never have dreamed that this popular ballad would one day lead to the creation of a much-needed addition to the English dictionary: 'mondegreen', the term for a misheard song lyric that changes the meaning of the original. It was coined in 1954 by American writer Sylvia Wright, who related in *Harper's Magazine* how, as a child, she had unwittingly turned the last words of the line 'They have slain the Earl o' Moray and *laid him on the green* into '… and Lady Mondegreen'.

Donibristle House was rebuilt in the early 18th century, but burned down again in 1858. Some of the remains were incorporated into a luxury apartment block in 1997, but the once elegant mortuary chapel, burial place of nine Earls of Moray, lies derelict and neglected, hemmed in by modern housing. Though it postdates the Bonny Earl's last day by 140 years, it's hard not to imagine him there as you contemplate the noble ruin in its verdant enclave. Those with a mischievously romantic streak will surely be able to picture Lady Mondegreen too, lying by his side, faithful unto death.

Address Donibristle Chapel, off River Walk, Dalgety Bay, KY11 9YF | **Getting there** Bus 7B, X57 or X58 to Moray Way (Oxcars Drive), a short path between nos. 5 & 7 River Walk (NB not River View!) leads up to the chapel | **Hours** Viewable from the outside only | **Tip** Denis Carbonaro's Bark Park, a mile north-west, is a surreal mini-theme park in a Dalgety Bay garden, featuring a tree-top galleon, woolly mammoth and outsize spider, all made largely from branches and recycled wood (132 Strathbeg Drive, KY11 9XH, +44 (0)7882 430210; open daily).

9 The Abbey Church

How Tiffany finally got together with Bruce

The history-steeped church that dominates the heart of Dunfermline is, to coin a phrase, a building of two halves: a bright, airy, busy neo-Gothic parish kirk annexed to the silent, dark, cavernous space of Scotland's greatest Romanesque remnant. Queen Margaret chose the site in 1070 for a priory, which her son David I later replaced with a grand monastic church incorporating a mausoleum for Scotland's monarchs. The Reformation saw the building brutally stripped of its finery, but the vast nave continued to be used as a parish church, shored up in the 1620s by massive flying buttresses.

The rest of the abbey complex gradually crumbled, and in 1817 architect William Burn was engaged to build a new church on the site of the old choir, with the medieval nave relegated to the role of a vestibule. Then workmen clearing the ruins discovered a forgotten vault containing a gold-enshrouded body, thought to be that of Robert the Bruce, outlaw king of Scotland's First War of Independence, who had been buried there in 1329. Patriotic and civic pride were rekindled, and Burn's plans modified to include gargantuan stone letters spelling KING ROBERT THE BRUCE on a parapet round the tower. The royal remains were reinterred in the new church in 1819, and a memorial brass was added 70 years later.

In 1913 philanthropist Andrew Carnegie commissioned a stained-glass window from the renowned Tiffany Studios of New York, to be installed in the church as a memorial to his family. Thirty years earlier he had paid for a new west window, but this dreamy, secular design, of a flowery sunset landscape in Art Nouveau style, was deemed by the administrators to be an 'anachronism' and 'inharmonious with the rest of the edifice'. It was only in 2019, after decades spent in storage and as a feature of the local Carnegie Hall, that the newly restored Tiffany window – a stunning example of his patent Favrile technique – was finally accepted, with due ceremony, by its long-intended home.

Address St Margaret Street, Dunfermline, KY12 7PE, +44 (0)1383 723005, www.dunfermlineabbey.com | Getting there Train to Dunfermline Town or bus to Dunfermline Bus Station; enter the church from the transept door at the north-east | Hours Apr–Oct, Mon–Sat 10am–4.30pm, Sun 2–4.30pm | Tip The church has a small exhibition about Robert the Bruce, including a 3-D virtual reconstruction of his tomb and a cast of his skull. Note that the ancient nave – a fabulously atmospheric space – has a separate entrance, and is administered as part of the Palace complex (see ch. 15).

10 Abbot House

An old survivor, in the pink once more

The cheery glow of Dunfermline's much-loved 'pink hoose' gives it a distinctive presence on the narrow wynd of Maygate. Just yards from the Abbey Church and incorporating part of its precinct wall, the rambling historic residence began life around 1450, probably as the abbot's lodging, and was extended over the following two centuries. In 1624, its solid stone construction enabled it to survive a conflagration that, in the space of four hours, destroyed an estimated nine-tenths of Dunfermline's houses. It stands today as the oldest domestic building in the town, with a long, chequered history of occupancy including periods as an iron foundry, an art school and a training centre for pilots fighting the Luftwaffe.

The rose-tinted harling was added in the 1990s as part of an extensive programme of refurbishment to develop Abbot House as a heritage centre. Curator Elspeth King took on the challenge of creating a museum without a historic collection by transforming the interior into a work of art in its own right. Artists and craftspeople were employed to contribute to displays interpreting the history of the town and of the building itself in an imaginative and dynamic way. Original murals, including 16th-century fragments with scenes from Virgil's *Aeneid*, were complemented by new wall decoration, most notably a large ceiling painting, *The Thistle of Dunfermline's History,* by renowned artist and writer Alasdair Gray. A formal garden was created in homage to a former resident, the 17th-century herbalist and writer Anne Halkett, and there was a popular café. In 2015, Abbot House was forced to close due to funding difficulties, but within four years grants had been secured for a phased programme of renovation and redevelopment. The building has now reopened as a cultural hub, with a focus on social interaction, learning and creativity. Attractions include a gift shop featuring items by local makers and a new café with seating in the garden, plus craft studios, workshops and events – and a World War II Escape Room.

Address Maygate, Dunfermline, KY12 7NE, www.abbothouse.org | **Getting there** Train to Dunfermline Town or bus to Dunfermline Bus Station | **Hours** Gift shop and café: Tue–Fri 10am–4pm, Sat 9am–5pm | **Tip** Above the entrance door is an inscription in Middle Scots: 'SEN VORD IS THRALL AND THOCT IS FRE/KEIP VEILL THY TONGE I COINSELL THE' – in other words, think what you like but be careful what you say. The motto is based on lines from the 15th-century poem *The King's Quair*, a love allegory attributed to King James I.

11 Andrew Carnegie Birthplace Museum

The noblest possible use of wealth

'Congratulations, Mr Carnegie – you are the richest man in the world.' These were the words of financier J.P. Morgan when, in 1901, he handed over a cool $400 million – £163 billion in today's money – for the US steel empire of Dunfermline's most famous son. Andrew Carnegie went on to become the world's greatest philanthropist, giving away 90 per cent of his wealth for the benefit of others. He was just 13 when he and his family were forced by poverty to emigrate to the USA, but the ethics that shaped his life had their origins in his early years in Dunfermline. Young Andrew began work in Pennsylvania, first as a bobbin boy in a textile mill and later as a telegraph messenger. He'd had just five years of schooling, but was an avid reader, and the books he borrowed from a wealthy man's private library became the tools of the self-improvement that drove his later success as an entrepreneur, as well as the self-analysis that made him question the purpose of the accumulation of wealth. He came to believe that education was the key to transforming society by helping people to help themselves, and the 2,811 public libraries he funded around the globe are among his many enduring legacies.

The weaver's cottage where Carnegie was born in 1835 is now a museum which, along with the adjoining memorial hall, tells the remarkable and at times controversial life story of the 'star-spangled Scotchman' in a way that's informative and absorbing for all ages. Recently redeveloped with eye-catching displays and lively interactives, it's become a popular family attraction, with activities featuring everything from eight-year-old Andrew's rabbit-based business venture to the superstar dinosaur he later used to promote world peace. There's even a cameo appearance from four residents of Sesame Street, created with funding from the Carnegie Corporation.

Address Moodie Street, Dunfermline, KY12 7PL, +44 (0)1383 724302, www.carnegiebirthplace.com | Getting there Train to Dunfermline Town or bus to Dunfermline Bus Station | Hours Daily 11am–4pm | Tip Though it may not have the cachet of its more famous New York counterpart, Dunfermline's Carnegie Hall is no less worthy of a visit. A venue for music, drama, comedy, dance and children's shows, it was built in the 1930s and retains many original Art Deco fittings (+44 (0)1383 602302, www.onfife.com).

12 The City Chambers
A ubiquitous clock and a hungover elf

When Provost Kenneth Mathieson commissioned a new home for transacting Dunfermline Council's business in 1875, this ancient capital of Scotland was a community of fewer than 20,000 people. But thanks to its status in the linen weaving industry – Dunfermline damask was said to be unequalled in the world – it had gained rapidly in prosperity in the previous half century. Mathieson was the son of an architect, and must have had an idea of the sort of centrepiece he wanted for the town when he appointed Fife-born James C. Walker to come up with a fittingly ornate design. Based in Edinburgh, Walker had trained in the best architectural practices of the day, and was fully conversant with the prevalent grandiose style, with its mingling of Scottish Baronial and French Gothic influences.

The elaborate turreted steeple that surges up to a giddy height of 117 feet at the corner of the L-shaped edifice makes an unmistakeable statement of civic pride. It was originally intended to be 43 feet shorter, but was altered when the council decided to incorporate a four-faced clock that could be seen all over the town. There is a feast of glorious decorative stone carving in mock-medieval style along both frontages – the masons clearly had fun creating the ornate balconies, exotic foliage and in particular the confection of gargoyles, mythical beasts and grotesque heads.

A stolid bust of Robert the Bruce supports an oriel window on Bridge Street, while down Kirkgate a sorry-looking fellow with elfin ears, a Willie Winkie hat and a crushing headache bears the load of a corbelled stair. He's said to be a caricature of a heavy-drinking burgh official who gave the masons a hard time; they retaliated by immortalising him for posterity with a permanent hangover. The interior is equally rich in carved ornamentation, with a magnificent hammerbeam ceiling in the Council Chamber. It also houses a small collection of Scottish paintings, of exceptional quality.

Address Corner of Kirkgate and Bridge Street, Dunfermline, KY12 7ND | Getting there Train to Dunfermline Town or bus to Dunfermline Bus Station | Hours Normally viewable from the outside only; tours occasionally available – ask at reception. The chief rooms can be booked for weddings and functions. | Tip If you're in need of a healthy snack or just an indulgent treat, it's only a few minutes' walk to New Row, where there are three highly-rated cafés offering diverse specialities: 269 Vegan (www.269vegan.co.uk), Juniper Wine Café and Bottle Shop (www.juniperwinecafe.co.uk) and Treat Time dessert parlour (www.facebook.com/treattimefife).

13__Fire Station Creative
Deco landmark aflame with artistic enterprise

'Long life, loose fit' is a term used by architects to denote buildings that are easily adaptable to new uses once their original function is redundant. That concept didn't exist in 1934, when Dunfermline Town Council engaged James Shearer to design a new fire station, so it's all the more remarkable how neatly his vast, purpose-built, state-of-the-art facility lent itself to conversion, some 80 years later, into a stylish contemporary arts centre.

Shearer was a local architect who had already completed several prestigious projects in the town. For this landmark building he created an International Style brickwork edifice (described in the press as 'severely utilitarian') that shows the influence of Dutch modernist Willem Dudok in its prominent tower – publicly criticised at the time despite being an essential feature, used by firemen for hose-drying and ladder practice. The massive tripartite doorway was designed for quick getaway by the three large fire engines kept in the main hall; the ground floor also had a recreation room, control room and workshops, while the two upper floors were fitted out as living quarters for the firemen and their families. It served its purpose commendably for many decades, until in 2010 the Fire Service relocated to new premises at Pitreavie.

The fire station was on the 'at risk' register when enterprising artist Ian Moir, on the hunt for a building that would provide much-needed facilities for the local creative sector, realised its potential as a virtually ready-made arts centre. The funds required were fairly modest by construction industry standards, and his project soon received enthusiastic backing from many quarters. The charitable enterprise of Fire Station Creative opened its doors in July 2015, with a flexible exhibition space, 20 studios, an airy café and a classroom that now offers popular courses in everything from upholstery to comic-book art for kids.

Address Carnegie Drive, Dunfermline, KY12 7AN, +44 (0)1383 721564,
www.firestationcreative.co.uk | **Getting there** Train to Dunfermline Town or bus to
Dunfermline Bus Station | **Hours** Gallery & café: Wed & Thu 10am–5pm, Fri & Sat
10am–midnight, Sun 11am–4pm; for timetable of classes see website | **Tip** Details
of all the visual artists based in the building are on display; their studios can be visited
by appointment, or on twice-yearly open days. There are regular free music sessions in
the café on Fri and Sat from 9pm, as well as occasional ticketed performances.

14_Pittencrieff Park
Sweetness, light and peacocks

In all the panoply of gifts that Andrew Carnegie gave to the world, the one that meant most to him was the donation of Pittencrieff Park to the people of Dunfermline in 1903. The industrialist and philanthropist (see ch. 11) was born within sight of the Glen, as it's known locally. It was a ruggedly beautiful landscape, steeped in history and romantic legend, and from the glimpses young Andrew had it seemed 'as near to paradise' as anything he could imagine. However, the land was then private property; its owner grudgingly allowed access to local residents on one day of the year, but Andrew and his family were denied even that, due to the political activities of his Chartist grandfather and uncles. So it gave him particular delight when he was able to buy the estate and fulfil his long-held ambition to turn its 76 acres into a recreational space open to all, bringing 'sweetness and light' to the lives of ordinary people.

Step through the ornate gateway (named in tribute to Carnegie's wife Louise) at the end of the High Street, and within minutes you can be strolling in the wooded tranquillity of the Tower Burn gorge, with its waterfalls and wildlife, or enjoying the glories of the glasshouses, the Laird's Garden and other diverse plantings, all enhanced by major recent restoration. There are sweeping vistas down to the Forth as well as striking views of the historic Dunfermline skyline; other attractions include medieval sites associated with Malcolm Canmore and William Wallace, and a beautifully restored static steam locomotive of the type known as a pug, enjoying retirement after a long working life in the collieries of Central Scotland.

Since 1905, Pittencrieff has been home to much-loved colonies of peacocks (or more properly peafowl), which roam freely around the town centre as well as the park. The population almost died out after the demise in 2017 of 20-year-old Clive, but it has since recovered with new stock, including some rare white pea-chicks.

Address Bridge Street, Dunfermline, KY12 8QH | Getting there Train to Dunfermline Town or bus to Dunfermline Bus Station | Hours Unrestricted | Tip In the west of the park is the 1930s Glen Pavilion, which houses a café and is also a popular, stylish venue for weddings. Nearby is a memorial bench dedicated to local musician Stuart Adamson, who died tragically in 2001. Adamson was a founding member of the Skids and Big Country, both of whom played at the Pavilion, and the bench is decorated with some of his best-known lyrics.

15 The Royal Guesthouse

From poor pilgrims to an ill-starred prince

'The King sits in Dunfermline toun/Drinking the blude-red wine': the opening lines of the medieval ballad *Sir Patrick Spens* are a well-known reminder that the burgh was once Scotland's capital (and indeed that the national tipple used to be claret). A remnant of the old royal palace survives on a steep and commanding site by Dunfermline Abbey – a great soaring wall of windows that gives a wistful hint of its former magnificence. It was King Malcolm III who first established Dunfermline as his seat in the mid-11th century. However, the key figures in the story of the royal residence are two foreign-born Scottish queens, separated by over five centuries: Malcolm's pious and civilising second wife, Margaret of Wessex, and Anne of Denmark, the neglected and spendthrift consort of James VI.

Around 1070, Queen Margaret established a new church in Dunfermline and invited a community of Benedictine monks to settle there. An important part of the religious foundation was the guesthouse – the provision of hospitality was a key tenet of monastic life. Margaret is recorded as having regularly served food and drink there to 300 poor individuals, many of whom would have been pilgrims *en route* to St Andrews (see ch. 110).

The complex grew in grandeur after her son David I transformed the church into an abbey; the guesthouse gained a dual role as a royal residence, and it was remodelled over the centuries in a style befitting its importance. After the Reformation, the monastery buildings fell into disrepair, but in 1589 they were granted by James VI to his new bride Anne. The queen had the former guesthouse redeveloped as part of a sumptuous courtyard palace, and it was here that her second son, the future Charles I, was born. Ill omens are said to have attended the birth of the sickly boy, who was slow in learning both to walk and to talk. His troubled reign as king of England, Scotland and Ireland led to civil war and his ultimate execution.

Address St Margaret's Street, Dunfermline, KY12 7PE, +44 (0)1383 739026, www.historicenvironment.scot | **Getting there** Train to Dunfermline Town or bus to Dunfermline Bus Station | **Hours** Apr–Sept, Mon–Sat 10am–5pm, Sun 1–5pm, Oct–Mar, Tue–Sat 10am–4pm; ticket includes admission to the Abbey nave | **Tip** Other impressive buildings in the complex are the gatehouse and the vast monastery refectory, with its traceried west window and atmospheric undercroft. Inside the Abbey, look out for the classical tomb of William Schaw, the master of works who remodelled Queen Anne's palace.

16 St Margaret's Cave

Simple royal retreat, with ample parking

In the corner of a car park in Dunfermline town centre is a low stone building that at first glance you might mistake for a public toilet – an impression belied when you spot the lettering on the side reading 'Saint Margaret's Cave'. Perhaps a quaint little charity shop, then? Wrong again. It is in fact the unlikely entrance to a rather startling prefabricated tunnel that leads 56 feet underground to a small, atmospheric rock-cut shrine, long associated with Scotland's first 'official' saint, the 11th-century Queen Margaret.

Margaret was a Hungarian-born princess of the House of Wessex, educated in England, whose family fled to Scotland after the Norman Conquest. Around 1070 she married King Malcolm Canmore, a widower some 16 years her senior, in Dunfermline; contemporary sources state that she was a far from willing bride, having planned to dedicate her life to religion. Instead, she devoted herself to the much-needed reform of both the Scottish church and the royal court.

Tradition has it that when the queen needed to be alone with her god, she used to retreat to a little cave in a wooded glen; the king is said to have had it 'improved' to apologise for jealously doubting her motives for going there. After Margaret's canonisation in 1250, it became a popular place of pilgrimage.

But in 1962 the town council in its wisdom decided to fill in the glen to create a car park, which would have buried the cave. There was a public outcry, and after a campaign organised by Rosyth architect James Stewart a compromise was reached, and a ventilated tunnel constructed so that it remained accessible. The visitor centre and refurbished cave – complete with a rather Disneyfied reimagining of the queen at prayer, plus evocative medieval background music, sung *a cappella* by local group Opus 8 – were finally inaugurated in April 1993, as part of the celebrations marking the 900th anniversary of Margaret's death. Sadly, Mr Stewart died just days beforehand.

Address Glen Bridge Car Park, Chalmers Street, Dunfermline, KY12 8DF, +44 (0)1383 602386, www.onfife.com | Getting there Train to Dunfermline Town or bus to Dunfermline Bus Station | Hours Apr–Sept, daily 11am–4pm | Tip A reliquary containing the shoulder bone of the saint can be seen in the Lady Chapel of St Margaret's R.C. Memorial Church (East Port, KY12 7JB). The relic was returned to Dunfermline in 2008 after an eventful history, having been kept for centuries in the Escorial in Madrid before passing into the care of Ursuline nuns in Edinburgh.

17__Tam o' Shanter
'And at his elbow, Souter Johnny'

We're all overly familiar with the Victorian public statuary type that still persists in our town centres – solemnly sober men in upstanding poses, set up as moral exemplars to the populace (whatever their true failings). So it comes as a refreshing novelty to make the acquaintance of this unrepentantly merry pair of drinkers, immortalised in stone nearly two centuries ago and now silently disturbing the peace of Dunfermline's heritage quarter. Larger than life in every sense, the convivial figures represent Tam o' Shanter, picaresque hero of Robert Burns' mock-epic poem of 1790, sitting with his pal Souter [cobbler] Johnny, happily 'bousing at the nappy' [drinking strong beer].

They are the work of the Lanarkshire-born Robert Forrest, a sculptor with little formal training who won great acclaim in the early 19th century for his statues inspired by literary works and historical events. Tam and Johnny were first displayed around 1832 on Edinburgh's Calton Hill, where Forrest had a temporary workshop and exhibition space, set up as part of a bid to promote public support for the completion of the unfinished National Monument (later dubbed 'Scotland's Disgrace'). Burns' characters were a popular subject at the time thanks to the success of a Tam o' Shanter group carved in 1828 by Ayrshire mason James Thom, whose characters were copied in miniature as Staffordshire pottery figurines.

Forrest's statues had a long sojourn in the gardens of Kirklands House, near Saline, before being acquired by Fife Council in 2010 for Dunfermline, to complement the Murison Burns Collection of books, prints and ephemera relating to Scotland's national bard, which is among the treasured holdings of the Carnegie Library. The jolly inebriates now form the centrepiece of the sunny garden next to the splendid new galleries, designed by Richard Murphy Architects, and completed in 2017 as an extension of the 1883 building, the first library endowed by Andrew Carnegie (see ch. 11).

Address Carnegie Library & Galleries, 1–7 Abbot Street, Dunfermline, KY12 7NL, +44 (0)1383 602365, www.onfife.com/dclg | Getting there Train to Dunfermline Town or bus to Dunfermline Bus Station | Hours Mon–Fri 10am–5pm, Sat 10am–4pm, Sun noon–4pm | Tip The galleries are a museum of Dunfermline in all but name, with vivid displays on local themes. The library's special holdings, viewable in the Reading Room by appointment, include medieval illuminated manuscripts as well as the treasures of the Murison Burns Collection.

18_ The Mercat Cross
A unicorn to believe in

It remains to be proven whether the roots of Inverkeithing date back as far as the Roman general Agricola's anti-Caledonian campaign of AD 84, but what is certain is that by the mid-12th century the community was sufficiently established to be granted a royal charter as a burgh. At the heart of all burghs was the mercat (market) cross, a status symbol indicating an official place for trading goods, as well as a focal point for townsfolk to witness proclamations, celebrate holidays and join in the popular entertainment of tormenting miscreants.

Inverkeithing's cross is one of the finest extant in Scotland. Though currently sited unobtrusively, it's soon to be relocated to a prominent position in the Market Square. A replacement for an earlier wooden column, it was erected around 1400 courtesy of Robert III's queen consort Annabella Drummond, who often resided in the town. (Annabella had been *de facto* ruler of the country since a riding accident had left the king a depressive invalid, who declared that he wanted only to die and be dumped in a dung-heap.) In 1688, year of the 'Glorious Revolution', the crucifix that had previously formed the cross's finial was symbolically replaced with a carving of a perky unicorn – the heraldic animal of Scotland – squatting on a faceted sundial. Our infantilising 21st-century culture has reduced this proud, untamed creature of myth to a pastel-shaded, long-lashed, simpering soft toy. But the unicorn was then a fierce and noble beast, strong, swift, pure and the natural enemy of the lion – symbol of England.

The elaborate sundial may seem a counterintuitive feature in a country where clear skies can never be guaranteed for long. In fact it's one of a great number made in Scotland in the 17th century, part of a craze for ever more sophisticated sculpted dials that go far beyond basic solar timepieces, probably linked with the beginnings of freemasonry. This fashion persisted for centuries; there's a showy neo-Gothic example dated 1878 at Crawford Priory, near Springfield.

Address Bank Street, Inverkeithing, KY11 1LR | Getting there Train to Inverkeithing or
bus 7, 87, 88, X57 or X58 to High Street | Tip Inside St Peter's Kirk on Church Street is
another gift from Queen Annabella – a font dating from c1398, carved with four rather hefty
angels grasping coats of arms. It was buried for centuries and so is unusually well preserved.
On your way there, look up at the 18th-century tolbooth in Townhall Street to see a charming
carved and painted representation of St Peter and a sailing ship on the burgh's coat of arms.

19__Devilla Forest
Shinrin-joku, secret lochs and squirrel-spotting

A walk in the woods is a proven tonic for the mind and body. Those who like to formalise such things refer to it as *shinrin-joku* – literally 'forest bathing' – a term borrowed from Japan, where the simple experience of spending time surrounded by trees has long been a cornerstone of health care and healing.

With 700 hectares of managed woodland criss-crossed by a network of paths, Devilla Forest offers endless scope for this free restorative therapy, plus a surprising variety of intriguing sights along the way. Devilla is a working forest dating mainly from the 1950s, planted over the ancient Tulliallan Estate and so blessed with a great deal more character than the average Forestry Commission site. The name has nothing to do with diabolical goings-on: the word Devilla, of Gaelic origin, actually means 'bad farmland'. However, the woods do conceal some rather spooky historic places, including a boulder with deep grooves legendarily cut by the apron strings of a 17th-century witch, and the poignant grave of three children who died of the plague in 1645. Much of the area's past has been documented by local historians Bob and Meg Smith, whose maps are dotted around the forest, marked with the sites of antiquities, some now evocatively overgrown. There are no fewer than four secret lochs, all of them havens for wildlife such as otters; seasonal residents of Moor Loch (illustrated) include great crested grebes, Canada geese and swans.

For many, one of the forest's chief attractions is the Red Squirrel Trail, a well-interpreted, waymarked route through tall Scots pines that sustain a thriving though elusive population of the tufty-eared little ginger charmers. This native species was once widespread in the UK, but is now greatly reduced in numbers and hard to spot outside the Scottish Highlands, due to the incursions on its habitat of its grey American cousins. First introduced to Dunfermline's Pittencrieff Park in 1919, greys are now established all across Fife.

Address Kincardine, FK10 4AS, www.forestryandland.gov.scot; the website has a leaflet with a map of walking routes | **Getting there** Join the Red Squirrel Trail at the Forestry Commission car park on the A 985 1 mile east of Kincardine; alternatively, bus 8/A/B, 28, X24 or X27 to Kincardine High Street, then walk to east end of Osborne Drive, FK10 4RZ, to join the path to Moor Loch | **Tip** The woodland around Ladybank is another place in Fife where there's a good chance of seeing red squirrels (if you're quiet and patient); South Annsmuir, north-east of Ladybank Station, is a hotspot.

20 Tulliallan Kirkyard

Emblems of trade and mortality

There's been an upsurge of interest in old Scottish churchyards in the past few years – and not only from sensationalising 'ghosties-and-ghoulies' tour operators. They're becoming increasingly valued as monuments of social history, and rich sources of information about the forgotten lives of ordinary parishioners. In the Scottish Lowlands, a distinctive type of figurative headstone evolved in the 17th and 18th centuries, with individually styled memorials that often incorporate emblems of the trade or profession of the deceased. This detail was possible because of the nature of the material used – sandstone, which is much easier to work than marble or granite, allowing local masons to express their creativity in what became a lively form of folk art.

The kirkyard of Tulliallan Old Parish Church in Kincardine has some of the finest surviving 17th- and 18th-century gravestones to be found in Scotland. It's also one of the best looked after collections, thanks to years of rescue work by local enthusiasts Bill Wolsey and Willie Anderson in reinstating fallen and sunken stones on the long-disused site. The church itself, built in 1675, was abandoned in 1832 and became a roofless shell, now restored to house a memorial garden. The closely packed headstones that surround it give a vivid picture of centuries of past life in this quiet village, once a prosperous trading port. Traditional emblems of mortality – skulls, crossed bones and hourglasses – are all around, often along with a heart to symbolise the soul. There is a preponderance of nautical imagery such as anchors, and a variety of ships at sail, as well as a splendid array of tools symbolising long-gone hammermen, farmers, leatherworkers, tailors, weavers and a whole host of other trades. Don't miss the charming headstone showing a woodcutter at work, near the east wall of the kirkyard. Once you become attuned to these evocative sculptures, you should find your visit life-enhancing, and even death-defying, as our ancestors would have done.

Address Wood Lea, Kirk Street, Kincardine, FK10 4PT | **Getting there** Bus X27 to Kincardine | **Hours** The key to the kirkyard gates is kept at Marco's Kitchen at 7 Kirk Street, open Mon–Fri 9am–3pm, Sat & Sun 10am–4pm (+44 (0)1259 730055) | **Tip** Marco's is a friendly little café with great home-made soups, snacks and cakes, and an entertaining owner. The excellent website of the Kincardine Local History Group has a map of the kirkyard and a catalogue of all the gravestones, plus details of their symbolism (www.kincardinehistory.com).

21 St Ninian's Land Art
Cosmic fragments of the art park that never was

Unprepared travellers zooming through Fife on the M 90 should be forewarned of a strange distraction just south of Junction 4 – the sudden glimpse of a colossal terraced mound with a trio of conical peaks and three brazier-like crowns. It could be a mysterious ancient monument from some parallel universe, but in fact it's a relic of recent date from the ill-fated Fife Earth Project, which was to have transformed the 269-hectare site of St Ninian's open cast mine into Scotland's biggest public artwork.

The ambitious scheme was initiated in 2003, when Scottish Coal commissioned world-renowned landscape architect Charles Jencks to create a vast landform sculpture out of the scarred and exhausted terrain. Jencks took the inspiration for his design from the profound contribution made by Scots to global history and culture; there were to be four enormous, differently shaped earthworks, representing the four continents settled by the Scottish diaspora, a loch in the shape of Scotland and a six-mile network of pathways, with scrapped mining equipment incorporated as sculptural features. But the scheme collapsed in 2013 when Scottish Coal's parent company went bust, with only the European mound complete and the Americas half constructed, and nature soon began to reclaim the blighted landscape. Plans to restore and redevelop the site have since come to nothing, though there is hope for a new proposal to repurpose it as an ecotourism destination.

The completed mound can be accessed either as originally intended, round a long processional spiralling path, or via an unofficial shortcut that leads into what Jencks termed a 'cosmic avenue' of repurposed pipe sections, digger scoops and engine wheels. Standing on the windy summit (now used as an adventure playground by local youngsters) is a thought-provoking and emotional experience, as you survey the vastness and eerie desolation of the abandoned site, and imagine the green swathes of the art park that might have been.

Address North of Loch Fitty, Kingseat, KY12 0SP | **Getting there** Bus 7B/D or 81 to Kingseat, walk north on Main Street (B 912) out of the village, take the path on the left signposted to Hawthorne Acres, then follow waymarkers for Fife Pilgrim Way. Cross the Loch Fitty causeway, then follow the second path on the left across a small bridge and go round a closed gate. You will soon see the mound ahead. | **Tip** Lassodie War Memorial stands in an isolated spot on the B 912, half a mile north of Kingseat. It was relocated from the lost village of Lassoddie, which fell into decline after mine closures and was demolished in the 1940s.

22 — The Vintage Bus Museum
Transports of delight

There's something about the sight, sound and even the smell of an old bus that inspires instant affection and a rush of nostalgia in just about everyone. You don't have to be an 'anorak' with an obsessive interest in the minutiae of specifications, routes, liveries and timetables to appreciate these sturdy egalitarian vehicles that once shuttled you to school and back, escorted you on your first date, or took you on your own magical mystery tours.

Founded in 1985, the Scottish Vintage Bus Museum has the largest collection of its type in Europe, with a fleet of nearly 200 passenger carriers housed on a 45-acre site at Lathalmond. (It's a nice coincidence that this is just down the road from the village immortalised by John Watt in 'The Kelty Clippie' – surely the world's only folk song about a bus conductress.) Most of the buses date from the 1920s to the 1980s, magisterial double-deckers and snub-nosed coaches, many with potent names redolent of ancient myths – Titan, Valkyrie, Atlantean, Olympian – or champions of the animal kingdom – Lion, Tiger, Cheetah, Leopard. Unmissable guest stars include a formidable 1930 steam roller, a cute 1963 bubble car and a resplendent Edinburgh horse tram dating from 1885, meticulously restored after decades languishing as a summerhouse in a Borders garden. The buses are almost all privately owned, lovingly renovated and maintained by members of the museum trust.

Opening to the public is restricted to Sunday afternoons; your ticket includes a bus tour of the extensive site, with enthusiastic volunteers to guide you round the exhibition hall, workshops and stores. There is also a specialist bookshop. On open days, trips outside the museum are on offer, and highly recommended: the experience of lurching along the byways of West Fife in a Leyland Victory Mark 2 double-decker, made by Alexander's of Falkirk for the China Motor Bus Company of Hong Kong, is quite unforgettably surreal.

Address M 90 Commerce Park, Lathalmond, Dunfermline, KY12 0SJ, +44 (0)1383 623380, www.svbm.org.uk | Getting there M 90 to Junction 4, then west on B 914 & B 915; bus: free shuttle service from Dunfermline Bus Station on event days only | Hours Apr – 1st week of Oct, Sun 12.30 – 5pm | Tip The Lathalmond Railway Museum is based in a locomotive shed nearby, formerly a Royal Naval Store Depot with an internal rail network, currently being restored by enthusiasts. Short rides on a brake van and other vehicles are available (Apr – early Oct, Sun 12.30 – 4pm; www.shed47.org).

23 — Lochore Meadows
From colliery wasteland to country park

With 1,200 acres of rolling countryside surrounding an expanse of shining water, the country park of Lochore Meadows appears to be a timeless natural environment. But in fact it's been shaped by centuries of human activity, which have even changed the position of the loch. In the 1790s the original Loch Ore was drained by the landowner to create fields for cultivation, though the land remained boggy. Then in the mid-20th century the exploitation of the area's deep coal seams led to subsidence and extensive flooding, creating a new body of water on the altered site.

Known locally as 'the Meedies', the much-loved park was created in the late 1960s and '70s out of a landscape devastated by the coal industry, in what was the largest reclamation scheme in Europe at the time. A million trees now thrive in the six-inch layer of topsoil that covers the heaps of mining waste left after the closure of the area's seven pits. Evidence of this industrial history would be quite hidden were it not for the skeletal 112-foot tower that stands out starkly against the lush greenery. Built a hundred years ago from reinforced concrete, it could pass for a vast constructivist artwork, though its true function was as the headframe at Shaft No 2 of the Mary Pit, transporting men and coal to and from the surface for 45 years. A memorial panel lists those who lost their lives there.

In 2018, the park's visitor centre was named in tribute to former miner and councillor Willie Clarke, who had a key role in the development of the Meedies as a recreational resource. It was he who insisted on the preservation of the Mary Pit winding tower as a proud monument, when many people wanted every trace of the mines removed. It's just a fraction of the legacy of this deeply principled man, a life-long communist who represented his community for 43 years. In 2016, he was awarded the Freedom of Fife – only the third time such an honour has been bestowed.

Address Crosshill, Lochgelly, KY5 8BA, +44 (0)1592 583343, www.lochoremeadows.org | Getting there Bus 19/A/B/D or 81 to Crosshill (Lochore Meadows) | Hours Unrestricted; visitor centre: daily, summer 8am–6pm, winter 8.30am–4pm | Tip The park offers a wealth of activities for all ages including water sports, mountain biking, golf, fishing and birdwatching. Information is available on wildlife trails and walks, ranging from an easy stroll round the ruined Lochore Castle to the rewarding climb up Benarty Hill, known as the Sleeping Giant. Motorhome owners can park for the night for a small charge.

24 Preston Island

Floating Bob's high-water mark

Rail travellers who look east while crossing the Forth Bridge to Fife are rewarded with alluring glimpses of four scattered islands, Inchgarvie, Inchcolm, Inchkeith and the Isle of May. But a world away from the ruined abbeys, wartime defences and wheeling seabirds of these rugged outcrops, the western reaches of the Forth estuary hide a much lesser-known islet. The tiny Preston Island is man-made, reclaimed from the tidal waters for an early industrial venture. And since it's now part of an artificial peninsula – a nature reserve of ash lagoons, landscaped out of waste dumped from Longannet Power Station – you don't even need a boat to take you there.

This latecomer to the firth was created around 1800 by local laird Sir Robert 'Floating Bob' Preston, a congenial *bon viveur* who earned his nickname during his time as a ship's captain with the East India Company, where his lucrative trading ventures helped restore the family fortunes. Back on his extensive estate at Valleyfield, he was inspired to emulate the engineering feat of Sir George Bruce, who had created an undersea colliery at nearby Culross some two centuries earlier (see ch. 6). Preston succeeded in sinking his own coal mines half a mile off the coast, and constructed fine sandstone buildings on the pocket of land housing a pumping engine, factories and workers' homes – all in order to manufacture salt. There were once saltworks all along Fife's Forth coast, from Culross to Crail; up to six tons of coal were needed to produce one ton of this valuable commodity, made by boiling sea water in cast iron pans. The Preston Island enterprise was successful, but it ended abruptly in 1811 when an explosion resulted in the death of several miners.

Preston himself died, aged 94 and worth a million pounds, in 1834. Saltworkers continued to lease his island until the 1850s when excise officers, alerted by the 'wrang reek' (wrong smell) from the chimneys, discovered it was being used to distil illicit whisky.

Address Low Causeway, Low Valleyfield, KY12 8HL | Getting there Bus 8 or 28 to Low Causeway (Veere Park), then a 30-minute walk. Go down Station Path, cross the railway and follow the signposted path, along the shore, then inland | Hours Buildings viewable from the outside only | Tip Take a close look at the limestone boulders on the edge of the shoreline – they're from Charlestown quarry and are full of fossilised sea creatures. Sir Robert's once magnificent estate is just north of High Valleyfield; the woodland still contains elements of the landscape designed by the great Humphry Repton.

25 The Forth Road Bridge

Walking in the air

The trio of bridges spanning the Firth of Forth make a uniquely spectacular southern gateway to Fife. To the east looms the Forth Bridge, a cherished Scottish icon whose massive cantilevers have carried the railway across the waterway since 1890, while the gracefully fanned cables of the acclaimed Queensferry Crossing, opened in 2017 as a seamless link for the M 90 motorway, gleam to the west. Between them, the Forth Road Bridge, once a proud symbol of British post-war achievement, stands like an aggrieved middle child, sidelined by its two showy siblings.

A road bridge across the mile and a half narrows was first mooted in the 1920s, to replace the ferry service instituted by Queen Margaret in the 11th century, though it was not until 1958 that the six-year project began to construct the longest suspension bridge outside the USA. In principle it's like a rope bridge, except that the ropes are a pair of giant steel cables. Each was formed by aerially spinning over 11,500 wires, strung across the estuary over two huge towers with distinctive bracing in the shape of the St Andrew's cross.

But premature ageing, due to the unforeseen volume and weight of traffic that passed over it in its first five decades, led to the bridge's recent closure to all motor vehicles apart from buses and taxis. This may appear an ignominious fate for its declining years, but it's also a timely godsend for the environmentally aware. Not only are bus schedules much improved, but the vast decrease in vehicles – cut from up to 80,000 per day to fewer than 800 – means that walkers and cyclists can now enjoy a quiet, leisurely outing on the paths alongside the suspended roadway, over 200 feet above the Forth. It's an exhilarating sensation, with stunning panoramas to behold, as well as the opportunity to appreciate the monumental scale and beauty of this 20th-century world wonder. Just be prepared for windy weather out there, and for the vibration when buses scoot past.

Address Firth of Forth, A 9000 south of North Queensferry, www.theforthbridges.org | Getting there South end: bus X51, X52, X54, X55, X56, X57, X58, X59, X60 or X61 to Forth Road Bridge; north end: train to North Queensferry. The footpaths/cycleways run along both flanks of the bridge | Hours Unrestricted | Tip The original 1938 road bridge over the Forth is upriver at Kincardine – a handsome state-of-the-art swing bridge operated by photoelectric cells. It's still in constant use today, although it no longer swings. Keen cyclists can complete a 'tour de Forth' involving both crossings.

26 The Harbour Light Tower
You too can be a keeper of the lamp

Dwarfed by the mighty behemoth of the Forth Bridge, the tiny domed lighthouse at North Queensferry harbour looks at first sight oddly out of place, like a fancy pepper mill dropped from some celestial table. But circumstances were very different when it was constructed in 1817. The Town Pier was then the northern terminal of what was by far the busiest water crossing in Scotland, the Queensferry Passage across the Firth of Forth, constantly plied by ferryboat traffic since it was established by Queen Margaret in the 11th century. The new purpose-built tower with its beaming signal was a significant aid to navigation, designed by the great lighthouse engineer Robert Stevenson so that it also illuminated the pier for passengers. But when the iconic railway bridge was opened in 1890, the light was made redundant. Its little house gradually fell into disrepair, until 2007, when the dedicated volunteers of the North Queensferry Heritage Trust began a lengthy project to restore it to full working order as the world's smallest operational lighthouse.

A narrow spiral staircase of 24 steps leads up to the lantern itself, a replica of Stevenson's original design comprising an oil-fuelled lamp and 21-inch parabolic reflector. The lamp is of a type developed in 1780 by Swiss chemist Ami Argand (the most influential inventor no one remembers), which produced a much brighter and cleaner flame than was previously possible. It would originally have burned whale oil, which had to be warmed to thin it before use; the tower is cleverly designed with a stove on the ground floor vented by a flue pipe that runs up through the stair column. Visitors are invited to light the lamp themselves and become a certified Honorary Keeper, after a short session on lighthouse procedures and optics, following in the footsteps of Princess Anne, who lit the flame at the reinauguration in 2010. It's a rare opportunity to get a tiny taste of a profession that still holds a romantic appeal for many people.

Fountain Lamp – cross section

Address Town Pier, North Queensferry, KY11 1LA, www.nqht.org | Getting there Train to North Queensferry and a short walk (NB very steep hill); bus from Ferrytoll Park & Ride to Battery Road | Hours Daily 10am–4.30pm, weather permitting; email nqhtinfo@gmail.com to check. Booking essential to light the lamp; only one visitor at a time can be accommodated | Tip Two minutes' walk away at 17 Main Street, the Wee Restaurant is a cosy and intimate bistro with creative Scottish cuisine, using quality local produce (www.theweerestaurant.co.uk).

27 Underwater Safari

Sharks overhead!

The sight of a 10-foot shark with ragged teeth and gaping maw glid-ing through the water right above your head is bound to evoke an immediate visceral response – though this may be modified when you learn that the species in question is the docile, non-aggressive sand tiger, and that the one with the curved fin who's just swum past is a rather elderly female known as Tinkerbell. She and six other equally magnificent specimens of her kind are the star attractions of Deep Sea World's Underwater Safari, where visitors are led through a 100-million-gallon tank of sea water filled with wondrous marine life by means of a transparent tunnel nearly 400 feet long. It's reas-suring to know that the acrylic sheets from which the passage is made are 2.5 inches thick; although the curvature reduces the apparent size of the sea creatures by one third, this doesn't diminish the thrilling sensation you get of becoming part of their world. For those who are inspired to get more literally immersed, diving sessions are available that guarantee genuinely close encounters with the sharks, rays and teeming shoals of fish – an unforgettable experience.

Opened in 1993, Deep Sea World was an inspired repurposing of the abandoned and flooded Battery Quarry on the North Queensferry peninsula, dramatically sited in the shadow of the Forth Bridge. The see-through underwater tunnel was the first of its type in the north-ern hemisphere, made using technology developed in New Zealand in the 1980s. Although it's the undeniable highlight, there's a great deal more aquatic life to fascinate in the other displays, from piranhas, poison frogs and snapping turtles to seahorses, bearded dragons and seals. Education, conservation, research and captive breeding are all key to the work of the aquarium, and there's a daily schedule of talks, feeds and demonstrations from the friendly and dedicated staff. Kids' birthday parties are also on offer, with the option of having greetings to your child displayed in the shark tank.

Address Deep Sea World, Forthside Terrace, North Queensferry, KY11 1JR, +44 (0)1383 411880, www.deepseaworld.com | Getting there Train to North Queensferry and short walk (NB very steep hill) or bus from Ferrytoll Park and Ride | Hours Daily 10am–5pm (may vary in winter) | Tip Rankin's Café, nearby at 4 Main Street, is a friendly, deservedly popular little place with freshly prepared food and an inventive menu including good kids' options (+44 (0)1383 616313).

28 The Dockyard Castle

Silent witness marooned amongst umbilicals

You can't miss the prominent notice outside Rosyth Castle. Its purpose, however, is not to welcome visitors to the historic site, but to issue a raft of warnings about security at the nearby port, and you will look in vain for any cheerier information boards illustrating life in an early Renaissance tower house. Though once a renowned and picturesque landmark (which caught the distinguished eye of J.M.W. Turner), this well-preserved stronghold is no longer visitable or even easily visible, having been engulfed long ago by the vast sprawl of Rosyth Naval Dockyard.

Built in the late 15th century for the Stewarts, Lords of Rosyth, the castle stands on what was once a rocky outcrop in the Forth, accessible at low tide via a causeway; all the land beyond and around has been reclaimed from the sea over the past century. Improvements were made in 1561 to mark the return of Mary, Queen of Scots from France – a crest in the courtyard is inscribed in her honour, and an old tradition claims that she stayed there in 1568 after her adventurous flight from Lochleven Castle.

In 1903, a tract of coastline including the castle was bought by the Admiralty, goaded by the arms race with Germany into constructing a new naval base on Britain's eastern seaboard. The original intention was to restore the tower as a library for officers, but this plan was postponed after the outbreak of World War I. The noble ruin then became a silent witness to the shipyard's many changes of fortune: mothballed in the 1920s, reactivated in 1939, later chosen to refit nuclear submarines and then involved in constructing the colossal *Queen Elizabeth*-class aircraft carriers. The site around the castle, now in private hands, is occupied by a company that supplies 'umbilical solutions' – high-tech subsea cables – to the oil and gas industry. The huge drums of colourful coils make a surreal backdrop to the stark and lonely ancient monument.

Address Livesay Road, Rosyth, KY11 2XB | Getting there From M 90 North Queensferry junction, follow signs to port of Rosyth and continue on B 981; bus to Ferrytoll Park & Ride, then a 20-minute walk west along King Malcolm Drive & Milne Road | Hours Viewable from the outside only | Tip Two minutes' walk away, just off the path through the wood beyond the railway line, is a fine 16th-century doocot (pigeon house) that once served the castle. On the lintel over the door is a carving of a snake (sadly damaged), a reference to the biblical exhortation 'Be ye … wise as serpents and harmless as doves'.

29 The 'Garden City'

Scotland's prototype new town

The ancient place name of Rosyth has been well known to Scots for over a century, thanks to the decision in 1903 to site a Royal Naval Dockyard there. However, the modern town that was built inland of the port to house its workforce attracts little interest today, despite having the distinction of being Scotland's one and only designated Garden City. Rosyth was originally planned according to the principles of a radical concept in urban planning, initiated in the 1890s by the writings of English visionary Ebenezer Howard. The essential aim of his Garden City movement was to create self-sufficient communities of low-density, good quality housing for workers in leafy settings, with parks, schools, churches, shops and other amenities at the centre, and an outer green belt separating homes from industry. In 1909, the radical Liberal Lord Shaw of Dunfermline declared the government's aim to make Rosyth 'a model town for the world'.

It was not until 1915 that its construction actually began; in the meantime, over 2,000 workers and their families, mainly from England, were lodged in 'Tin Town', a grim settlement of corrugated iron huts. Then, within four years, 1,600 new homes were built to the designs of A.H. Mottram, a pupil of pioneering Garden City architect Raymond Unwin. Laid out along wide tree-lined streets, they were cottages of a classic English vernacular type, with features then quite unfamiliar to Scots used to traditional tenements. All had front and back gardens – a much-admired novelty – though other imported elements, including some construction methods and materials, were criticised as unsuited to the local climate and later modified. But development stalled when the dockyard closed in 1926, and the town was never completed as planned. Although Rosyth as it stands may fall some way short of the utopian ideal, its role as a trailblazer for housing reform in Scotland should not be forgotten; its design credentials are reflected in hundreds of cities around the world.

Address The photo shows Rosyth Parish Church, 82 a Queensferry Road, KY11 2PQ, at the heart of the Garden City (www.rosythparishchurch.org) | **Getting there** Train to Rosyth; bus 7, X51 or X55 to Queen's Buildings | **Hours** The church's Heritage Café welcomes visitors, Tue 1.30–4pm | **Tip** The Gothenburg Hotel at 138 Queensferry Road was originally one of over 20 'Goth' pubs in Fife, set up in the early 20th century as part of a social programme to control heavy drinking. It retains many features of its Arts and Crafts interior.

30__ The Binn
Vanished history on the rocks

What's in a name? The small volcanic hill that rises protectively behind Burntisland lacks a romantic handle like that of its cousin across the water, Arthur's Seat: its blunt designation, the Binn, is simply a corruption of the Gaelic *bryn*, meaning 'hill'. Perhaps that has given it an image problem, for its lovely wooded heights seem curiously underappreciated today.

Glorious panoramas across the Firth of Forth can be enjoyed from the top, but that's not the only good reason for tackling the easy climb to its ridge. On the western slope is a recently discovered prehistoric site: an outcrop of rock pecked with carvings known as cup and ring marks, dating from at least 4,000 years ago. In 2003, a local man who had played there as a child realised their significance after a visit to an exhibition in Edinburgh. These hauntingly exquisite patterns, variants of concentric circles around a central hollow, are found in many places of ancient significance in the west of Scotland, but are very rare in Fife. Their original purpose must always remain enigmatic, though the sight of the Craigkelly radio mast nearby does make one ponder on the eerie similarity between these prehistoric ripples and the modern icon for a transmitter.

To the east of the ridge is a relic of much more recent and very different activity: the scant remains of Binn village, once a settlement of almost 100 houses, built for workers during the short-lived local oil boom that began in 1878 with the founding of the Binnend shale mine and oil works. At its peak it boasted a daily output of 15,000 gallons of crude oil, extracted from the rich seams of shale formed from the remains of mud-dwelling creatures of aeons past, and processed to make lamp oil, paraffin wax and fertiliser. The works closed in 1894, but the village lived on, first as accommodation for soldiers in World War I and later as holiday homes popular with city folk. Despite the lack of running water, it was not until 1954 that its last resident left.

Address Burntisland, KY3 0AJ | Getting there Train to Burntisland; bus X57 or 7. Cup and ring marks: follow Cowdenbeath Road (A 909) out of town to the footpath signposted to Standing Stanes Road. Go uphill until you reach a field, with a pond ahead to the left. Bear right, cross the fence into the wood and climb to the rocky outcrop. A small Scheduled Monument notice marks the site. Binn village: follow signposted footpath up the hill off Kirkcaldy Road (B 923), just beyond Dodhead Golf clubhouse. | Tip Burntisland Heritage Trust offers free, guided walks that include the Binn (Apr–Sept; www.burntisland.net), and also mounts illuminating exhibitions of local interest at 4 Kirkgate, KY3 9DB (late June–Aug, Thu–Sat 11am–4pm).

31__ The Kirk of the Bible

Four-square equality, and a better Good Book

With its octagonal belfry and gilded weathercock, the kirk that crowns the high bank overlooking Burntisland harbour makes a splendid landmark. But those who view it only from afar are missing out, as its interior is truly uplifting. This parish kirk is in fact one of the most remarkable churches in Scotland, both for its distinctive design and its place in history. Completed in 1595 and still in use today, it was among the first to be built after the Scottish Reformation, and its square plan, expressing the equality of all believers under the new order, is unique in the country. The pulpit is positioned just off-centre, so that the minister is surrounded by the congregation. Inevitably, some worshippers had to demonstrate that they were more equal than others: the delightful canopied pew in inlaid oak was installed in 1606 for the laird, and later served for local magistrates. Box pews known as pumfells were the province of the grander families, while merchants and members of craft guilds adorned the gallery where they sat with panels vividly painted with insignia, ships and nautical symbols.

The kirk has yet another distinction: shortly after its completion, a decision was taken within its walls that would have incalculable influence on the entire English-speaking world. On 12 May, 1601, the General Assembly of the Church of Scotland convened here in the presence of James VI, to escape the plague then raging in Edinburgh. On the agenda was the proposal to commission a new English translation of the Bible; the king readily agreed, and the motion was unanimously approved. It was not until three years later, after his coronation as James I of England, that work actually began, but the Authorised Version – still the most widely published text in the English language – had its genesis here in Fife. Its poetry (which owes much to the earlier translation of William Tyndale) still resonates for believers and atheists alike; millions quote from it unthinkingly every day.

Address Burntisland Parish Church, East Leven Street, Burntisland, KY3 9DL, +44 (0)1592 872139, www.facebook.com/burntislandparishchurch | **Getting there** Train to Burntisland; bus 7 or X57 | **Hours** Guided tours June–Aug, Thu–Sat 2–4pm; group visits available | **Tip** Burntisland Links is a wonderful green space that extends behind the long sandy beach. A traditional fairground is located here from May to August, and on the third Monday in July it's home to the second-oldest Highland Games in the world.

32 The Museum of Communication

Technology with knobs on

At a time when UK town centres seem locked in a spiral of decline, it's a joy to discover one that's bucking the trend. Burntisland's High Street is lined with impressively well-stocked independent traders, including an award-winning greengrocer, a fine fishmonger, two butchers and a zero-waste grocer. As a bonus you'll also find a museum devoted to a subject just as central to our modern lives as food: communications technology. It may sound impenetrable to the non-specialist, but the dedicated volunteer staff present the highlights of their collection of radios, gramophones, telephones, TVs, computers and the like in highly accessible displays that are anything but geeky.

What now comprises over 40 tonnes of artefacts and equipment had its beginnings in 1973, when electrical engineer Harry Matthews decided to restore a 1935 Ekco wireless he'd found in a dustbin. When he showed off the result at the Edinburgh University lab where he worked, he was inundated with donations of old radios, and by 1979 his collection had grown hugely in scope and volume, and was on display. After many vicissitudes, the Museum of Communication finally gained a permanent home in 2003 (sadly, three years after its founder's death) in a former ex-servicemen's club in Burntisland. A large proportion of the devices are, miraculously, kept in working order, thanks to their passionately knowledgeable volunteer technicians, and you may, for instance, have the privilege of listening to discs on a Polyphon music box from c1885. Hands-on exhibits include a replica of an optical telegraph system used in the Napoleonic Wars. There are also components from the room-sized LEO, the world's first business computer, made c1949 for J. Lyons' tearooms – all of which might make you reflect with mixed emotions on the multi-function slimline wizards that we each carry with us today.

Address 131 High Street, Burntisland, KY3 9AA, +44 (0)1592 874836, www.museumofcommunication.org.uk | Getting there Train to Burntisland; bus 7 or X57 | Hours Annual exhibition: Easter–Sept, Wed & Sat 11am–4pm; rest of year, Wed & Sat by appointment | Tip The house where scientist Mary Somerville (1780–1872) lived as a child and young woman is at 30/31 Somerville Square. A brilliant mathematician, astronomer and pioneer of women's education, she gave her name to Somerville College in Oxford.

33__ The Wemyss School of Needlework

Stitches in time

The community of Coaltown of Wemyss possesses a veritable hidden gem that defies expectations of a former mining village – a creative centre devoted to traditional hand-sewing techniques. A tree-shrouded cottage on Main Street has been the purpose-built home of the Wemyss School of Needlework for 140 years, yet thousands drive past every day without registering its presence, despite the elegant sign with its logo of a swan perched on a threaded needle.

Inspired by the example of London's Royal School of Needlework, the philanthropic Dora Wemyss decided in 1877 to organise her own courses to train the daughters of local miners as prospective seamstresses and ladies' maids. Under a series of exacting mistresses, the stitch-perfect work produced by pupils became widely renowned, and orders from prestigious customers for fine clothes and home furnishings flooded in for over half a century. But teaching ceased during World War II, and although the school continued as a supplier of materials and designs, the building slowly fell into disrepair, until the enterprising current guardian, Fiona Wemyss, took the helm in 2012. Now refurbished and modernised, the school is thriving once again as a source of tuition and fount of inspiration for anyone with an interest in needlework and its history.

Exquisite antique textiles from the collections of Wemyss Castle are on display, along with fascinating archive material. Specialist classes cover techniques from medieval Opus Anglicanum embroidery to contemporary needlepoint. The shop stocks a unique range of needlepoint kits inspired by the historic collection, including a rose, thistle and lily design associated with Mary, Queen of Scots, and bespoke kits can also be ordered, based on the dazzling array of patterns that line the walls.

Address Main Street, Coaltown of Wemyss, KY1 4NX, +44 (0)1592 651346, www.wemyssneedlework.com | Getting there Bus 7, 7A, X60 or X61 to Coaltown of Wemyss (Bowling Green) | Hours Wed, Thu & Sat 10am–5pm; group visits by arrangement. See website for details of classes | Tip The walled garden at nearby Wemyss Castle is home to an unofficial national collection of clematis, among other horticultural wonders (www.wemysscastlegardens.com; mid-Apr–July, Mon–Fri 9.30am–6pm, by prior appointment only: phone +44 (0)1592 652181 or +44 (0)7825 151479).

34_ The Wemyss Caves
Threatened traces of the painted people

Caves have always had a powerful fascination for human beings wherever in the world they occur, and Fife is no exception. The coastal district of Wemyss, home to a series of caverns hollowed out by the sea from the red sandstone cliffs, owes its name to the Gaelic for 'cave', *uiamh*. But the Wemyss Caves were clearly a place of significance long before Gaelic speakers settled the area, for on their walls are a unique collection of enigmatic symbols engraved over 1,500 years ago by the Picts – one of ancient Europe's most intriguing lost peoples, on a par with Italy's 'mysterious Etruscans'. They first appear as *Picti* in a Roman chronicle of AD 297; it's assumed that the name derives from the Latin for 'painted people', though recent scholarship disputes this. But whether or not they used to decorate their own skin, it's for their art that the Picts are remembered, in particular their strikingly fluent symbolic carvings, found chiefly on monumental stones and only rarely in caves. Little else survives as a record of their society, which once covered most of Scotland north of the Forth.

Symbols characteristic of Pictish art – abstract motifs and animal imagery – were first recorded in the 1860s in five of the Wemyss Caves, though only three of these can still be visited. Since their identification at least 25 carvings, including a fine example of the strange 'Pictish Beast', have been lost due to coastal erosion, rock falls and vandalism; all of these remain serious threats today, despite the caves' supposedly protected status as a scheduled ancient monument.

In 1986, concerned local volunteers formed the Save the Wemyss Ancient Caves Society, whose valiant work in preservation and education now includes curating a visitor centre and museum, and providing free guided tours in the summer. The Society also has an excellent website and online shop – their hand-knitted hats with Pictish Beast motifs are particularly recommended. Time is running out for the Wemyss Caves; see them while you still can.

Address Caves: path east of Weavers Court, East Wemyss, KY1 4SF; visitor centre: Terras Hall, The Haugh, East Wemyss, KY1 4SB, www.wemysscaves.org | **Getting there** Bus 7, 7A, X60 or X61 to East Wemyss (School Wynd) | **Hours** Caves: unrestricted; visitor centre: Apr–Sept, Sun 1.30–4pm; cave tours at 2pm and 2.30pm (booking essential) | **Tip** Perched on a cliff above the caves is Macduff's Castle, an atmospheric ruin traditionally associated with the Thane of Fife famed from Shakespeare's 'Scottish play'.

35 The Caichpule

Favourite court of the Queen of Scots

'The sport of kings' is an old idiom that has been applied to various pursuits, including the ever-popular regal pastime of going to war. But for royalty in 16th-century Scotland, the modish leisure activity was caich, the 'chasing game', a racquet sport imported from France. It was known there as *jeu de paume* (palm game), recalling its origins as a form of handball. In England the word 'tennis' had caught on, derived from the French *tenez* ('take heed!'), which is what serving players yelled to their opponents long before they resorted to grunting. Nowadays it's called real, or royal tennis, to distinguish it from the upstart lawn tennis, which came in around 1870. And it's very much a court game in another sense, as it requires a special walled and paved enclosure, once known as a caichpule.

The oldest tennis court in the world still in regular play is the caichpule at Falkland Palace (see ch. 36), built in 1539–41 for James V, as part of his transformation of the royal residence in French Renaissance style. His daughter Mary, Queen of Scots became a keen player here; her practice of donning men's breeches to allow herself freedom of movement no doubt added to her flighty reputation. In those days servants would have served the first balls, to preclude the need for any undignified bending on the part of their masters.

The caichpule preserves unique features not found in other surviving courts, notably the four openings or 'lunes' in the wall at the service end, plus the absence of a roof. Since 1975 the dedicated members of the Falkland Royal Tennis Club have kept the game alive within its walls, mastering the arcane rules as well as the strokes required to get a spin out of the solid, heavy ball with the short, asymmetrical racket. The club welcomes visiting players, but even those with no wish to try their backhand will find this a highly atmospheric spot, especially in summer, when the spectators' gallery resounds with the shrill flitting of the swallows that have nested there for generations.

Address Falkland Palace, East Port, Falkland, KY15 7DA | Getting there Bus 36, 64 or 66/A to Falkland (Palace); tennis court access is through a doorway in the palace garden, near the lily pond | Hours Palace garden: Mar–Oct, daily 11am–5pm; Royal Tennis Club sessions: Sun from 10.30am, Wed from 5pm (2pm in winter); see www.falklandtennis.wordpress.com | Tip The lovely palace gardens feature a giant chess board, where those who prefer less energetic games might enjoy trying their skills. In the orchard is a figure in woven willow by Trevor Leat, which captures the spirit of Queen Mary.

36 Falkland Palace
Reimagined Renaissance splendour

'The kings of Scotland had more fine palaces than most princes in Europe': thus wrote Englishman Daniel Defoe, in his pioneering 1720s travel guide to the past glories of the newly united Great Britain. He noted in particular the resplendent palace at Falkland, 'once the most in request of all the royal houses in Scotland' and in Defoe's opinion one of the very few sights in the county of Fife to merit a detour inland. The great historic residence sank into a long period of decline shortly after his visit, but its second life began in 1887 when John Crichton Stuart, third Marquess of Bute, became its hereditary keeper. One of the richest men in the world, and a passionate antiquarian, Bute was responsible for a vast restoration scheme which, though never completed, recreated parts of the interior in the imaginary splendour of its 15th- and 16th-century heyday.

Now in the care of the National Trust for Scotland, Falkland Palace remains a 'must-visit', redolent of the royal intrigues and pastimes of a distant era, richly embellished with the trappings of nostalgic Victorian romanticism.

Long before it became the favourite country retreat of the Stewart monarchs, the land was occupied by a hunting lodge; this grew into a castle of the powerful Macduff Earls of Fife, which witnessed some grimly notable episodes before being commandeered by the crown in the early 15th century. By 1458 it was officially a palace, and in 1500 the grand quadrangle started to take shape under the direction of Scotland's first true Renaissance king, James IV. Its refashioning in the continental manner began in 1537, achieved by French master masons employed by James V, working alongside their Scottish counterparts in a creative fusion. Among their triumphs is the formidably massive gatehouse, whose conical-roofed towers effortlessly dominate the delightful main street and rather less assertive historic homes of the old village of Falkland.

Address East Port, Falkland, KY15 7BY, +44 (0)1337 857397, www.nts.org | Getting there Bus 36, 64 or 66/A to Falkland (Palace) | Hours Mar–Oct, daily 11am–5pm | Tip In 1970, Falkland became the first village in Scotland to be designated as a conservation area. The highly atmospheric old burgh preserves its medieval layout, with traditional 17th-century houses, grand and humble, lining its streets and wynds; 28 of its buildings are officially listed as being of historic importance.

37 Maspie Den
Walk behind the water

'Den' is an old Scots word for a narrow, wooded gorge with a rushing stream at the bottom – equivalent to the English 'dell' or 'dingle'. Fife boasts several such places, which offer soothing walks to the accompaniment of babbling brooks – but there's only one that also features the opportunity of a close encounter with a gushing cascade. The path round Maspie Den takes you right behind the Yad waterfall: its proportions depend on the recent rainfall, though they're never exactly Niagaran. But lingering under the glistening rocky overhang, as the foaming spout before you tumbles ceaselessly into the burn below, is a truly exhilarating experience for all the senses.

The Maspie Den footpath is one of a network of walking routes on the vast pleasure grounds of the Falkland Estate, leading round what's confusingly called a 'designed' landscape. Natural forces were clearly responsible for the configuration of the gorge, which was created around 13,000 years ago, at the end of the last Ice Age; however, it was an academic, Professor John Bruce, who undertook the task of making it more picturesque and accessible, as part of the extensive programme of improvements he made after purchasing the estate in 1821. His work in Maspie Den, which included tree planting, bridge building and path construction, was continued after his death by his wealthy Eurasian niece Margaret and her impecunious Bristol-born barrister husband Onesiphorus, who took the surname Tyndall-Bruce. The route up to the Yad waterfall, finally completed in the early 1830s, includes a substantial tunnel cut through a rocky outcrop that confronts you midway. (There's light at the end once you step inside – never fear!)

If you want to explore further, carry on up to the vantage point of the ruinous Temple of Decision, constructed by Onesiphorus as a retreat and place for contemplation. Based on the classical Temple of Theseus in Athens, it has now been partially restored.

Address Falkland Estate, KY15 7AF, +44 (0)1337 858838, www.falklandestate.co.uk | **Getting there** Bus 36, 64 or 66/A to Falkland (Palace), then a 10-minute walk west, along High Street and on to the Stables café and shop (10am–4pm; maps available). Continue to the wood, then follow the central road, ignoring tracks on either side. The path to Maspie Den is indicated on boulders (c1.5 hours there and back). For online map see www.fifecoastandcountrysidetrust.co.uk | **Hours** Unrestricted | **Tip** The estate's enterprising Stewardship Trust runs a programme of activities and events for all ages; see website.

38 Pillars of Hercules

Organic food pioneer still going strong

There is some disagreement among classical scholars regarding the details of the original pillars of Hercules – including their exact nature, location and what the muscle-bound lad actually did with them. Fifers, however, have no such doubts about their own 'Pillars' – an organic farm, shop, café and more besides, just outside Falkland. It's such a well-loved institution that locals dispense with the mythical hero's name when referring to it. Just to set the record straight, Hercules never did come to Fife, except in the imagination of the classically-minded Onesiphorus Tyndall-Bruce (see ch. 37), the 19th-century landowner who dreamed up the name for one of the boundary points of his extensive estate.

Pillars of Hercules was one of Scotland's first organic farms, established in 1983 by Bruce Bennett, a soil scientist trained in West Wales and inspired by the pioneering ecological movement there. Together with his wife Judy, an experienced Fife vegetable-grower, he expanded the modest venture over the decades into a bustling enterprise, without ever losing sight of the original ethos of sustainability. They now cultivate about 12 acres, with polytunnels growing salad leaves, tomatoes, courgettes and other vegetables; there's also an apple orchard, and laying hens. The organic farm shop, housed along with the deservedly popular vegetarian café in a charming rustic cabin, was recently judged the best in the UK for its truly exceptional range and quality. Herb and salad plants, flowers and ornamentals are also on sale, or you can pick your own.

If the legendary Hercules ever does drop by, he could do worse than stock up on Pillars' tasty range of homegrown leafy green veg – after all, look what spinach did for Popeye. The actual pillars, by the way, are far from Herculean; they're simply two short rough-hewn stone posts, where coffins used to be rested during funeral processions, on the way to the old burial ground at Kilgour.

Address Pillars of Hercules, by Falkland, KY15 7AD, +44 (0)1337 857749, www.pillars.co.uk | Getting there Bus 64 A to Pillars of Hercules | Hours Daily, shop 9am–6pm, café 9am–5pm (plus occasional bistro nights with live music) | Tip The farm has a holiday cottage available to let – a comfortable converted bothy (sleeps 4) that was used as a Home Guard shelter during World War II; details on website. There's also a campsite. Woodland walks are nearby and there is easy access to the Lomond Hills.

39 __ The Violin Shop

An ex-tec with more than one string to his bow

The antiques trade is not what it was. Today's avid collectors and casual rummagers prefer to do their browsing online, and the Aladdin's caves of yore have all but disappeared from our towns. It's a rare treat nowadays to find an old curiosity shop with a specialist proprietor on any high street, let alone in the heart of the stunning conservation village of Falkland.

Bob Beveridge opened his Violin Shop over 40 years ago. He began collecting stringed instruments as a lad in the 1950s, after his family inherited a house in Kingskettle with its contents – including a roomful of old cellos and violins. Bob's first career was in the Fife Constabulary, which he joined aged 19, later being seconded to the Scottish Crime Squad. Fifteen years and several harrowing murder investigations later, he'd had enough of the gruelling life of police detective, and decided to turn his old hobby into a new profession.

Apart from a host of stringed instruments, he keeps a stock of other collectibles, including a nice line in 'wally dug' pottery figurines. Bob never learned to play the violin himself, but he's a keen guitarist, despite having sustained a broken finger many years ago in his other hobby of hill racing. He can often be found strumming the guitar given to him by Roseanne, daughter of country music legend Johnny Cash, a friend since she first visited Fife to pick up on her late father's research into his ancestry. Bob had in fact become acquainted with Johnny some years earlier, when the 'Man in Black' came in search of his forebears from Strathmiglo after a chance meeting on a plane with the hereditary Keeper of Falkland Palace. More recently, the Violin Shop has been used as a location for the TV series *Outlander*, in which the centre of Falkland serves as the Highland city of Inverness in the mid-20th century. Bob wryly recalls the first day of shooting, when a wad of banknotes was stuffed into his hand simply for removing a sign from his shopfront window.

Address High Street, Falkland, KY15 7BU, +44 (0)1337 858181/+44 (0)7500 625069 | **Getting there** Bus 36, 64 or 66/A to Falkland (Palace); the shop is just beyond the fountain in the High Street | **Hours** Daily, according to Bob | **Tip** A minute's walk away, the Hayloft Tearoom is a good spot for a light lunch or afternoon tea; try the home-baked scones (Back Wynd, KY15 7BX, +44(0)1337 857590).

40 — The Bunnet Stane

Aeolian sculpture from aeons past

No one can say for sure how long the outcrop known as the Bunnet Stane (Bonnet Stone) has been so called, but it seems a rather commonplace tag to give to this timeless natural wonder. (The bunnet in question, it should be explained, is a flat, floppy woollen cap that was for centuries the everyday headgear of ordinary Scotsmen.) Others see it, almost as prosaically, as resembling a giant mushroom, but our ancient forebears must surely have had a suitably awe-inspiring name for such an extraordinary landmark. The term that geologists use for formations of this kind, Aeolian sandstone, is more appropriately respectful, deriving as it does from the Ancient Greek god Aeolus, keeper of the winds, and a dab hand at freeform sculpture when he put his mind to it.

Though it's hard to envisage when you look out over the lush Fife farmland, this area was once part of a hot, arid, wind-whipped desert, dotted with shallow, ephemeral inland seas. That was from around 353 to 415 million years ago, when what is now Scotland lay close to the Equator – a very long time before any Fifers, bunnet-clad or otherwise, came on the scene. The Bunnet Stane outcrop was formed from layer upon layer of sand, laid down by ancient shifting dunes, containing deposits of shells and silt that made its calciferous sandstone more resistant to erosion than the surrounding rock. It took aeons of weathering, by ice, water and the ever-changing winds to create the spectacular formation that we see today.

On the opposite flank of the outcrop is a large, naturally circular aperture, just above a carefully hewn man-made cave. Known as the Maiden's Bower, or Maiden Bore, it is linked variously to an ancient means of proving virginity, a legendary young woman whose lover was murdered here and, more tamely, a 19th-century geological survey. It's said that the rock-cut chamber was once used by hermits, and more recently by shepherds as a bothy.

Address Accessed from the car park on Dryside Road, near Gateside, KY14 7RR | **Getting there** Bus 66 to Gateside (Primary School) then follow Station Road and turn right at the T-junction. From the car park, follow a farm track (signposted) for 0.75 mile, a steady climb up to the lower slopes of West Lomond. | **Tip** You could continue with an ascent of West Lomond, but this should only be attempted by well-prepared, experienced hillwalkers with half a day to spare. An easier route to the summit can be followed from the car park on the east side of the hill at Craigmead, KY6 3HH.

41 Prehistoric Balfarg
A time before this

Planned in the late 1940s as Scotland's second new town, Glenrothes was to be built on a greenfield site: save for a few hamlets and country estates, the land that would provide thousands of new homes appeared to be virgin territory as far as human occupation was concerned. It was not until 1970 that an archaeological investigation in the north-east of the town, prior to the construction of a trunk road, began to reveal evidence that this was far from the case. As excavations continued in advance of house building at Balfarg, it became clear that this district had in fact been a very important gathering place in prehistoric times, constructed by some of the earliest farmers to inhabit Scotland, and revered for over two thousand years.

The ancient site has been all but destroyed by the relentless encroachment of our Anthropocene epoch, though three key features have been partially reconstructed. An arrangement of modern wooden posts marks the position of the oldest, a timber structure in the shape of a communal longhouse. Dating from around 5,700 years ago, this was a mortuary enclosure, a sacred place where bodies were left on high, raised platforms to be defleshed by birds and the elements. A short way to the west is the vast ring-shaped ditch of a henge monument, a major ceremonial centre now quaintly incorporated into a housing estate, while across the main road in Balbirnie Park are the remains of a stone circle, moved from its original location to make way for the mighty A 92.

We will never know what went on in the countless gatherings and rituals that took place here, though customs clearly changed with successive generations. The Balfarg excavations did, however, yield evidence from over 5,000 years ago of the use of henbane, a powerful hallucinogen. As you try to sense the former grandeur of these temples and tombs in the midst of the remorseless modern townscape, you may feel in need of a similar potion yourself.

Address The Henge, Balfarg, Glenrothes, KY7 6XU | **Getting there** From the A 92 in the north of Glenrothes take the B 969 and proceed west to Coul Roundabout. Take the first exit, then turn left on to Kilmichael Road, which loops round the street that encircles Balfarg Henge. For the mortuary enclosure follow the short path leading east into the woods, near the bus stop for Glengarry Court. For Balbirnie stone circle, cross the A 92 at the pedestrian crossing and turn right into the park. | **Tip** The nearby Georgian mansion of Balbirnie House is a luxury country house hotel set in 400 acres of parkland. Henbane is not available, but a champagne afternoon tea in the orangery makes a fine alternative (www.balbirnie.co.uk).

42 __ The Town Art
A regular army of hippopotami

A huge hippopotamus stands broodingly on a pavement in Glenrothes town centre, as if preparing to trot across the road and raid the M&S Foodhall. No one bats an eyelid: local folk have a special relationship with his kind. Public artworks have been part of life here for over 50 years, and more than 170 pieces are now sited throughout the town. This latest, remarkably life-like addition – made from recycled scrap metal by blacksmith-artists Rory and Kyran Thomas – is a homage to the troops of concrete hippos that appeared in the mid-1970s, much-loved 'play sculptures' that came to be adopted as mascots of Glenrothes.

The original hippos were designed by Stanley Bonnar, a young assistant of David Harding. Appointed in 1968, Harding was the first artist in the UK to be given a long-term brief of collaborating with architects, engineers and builders in the creation of a planned new town. This was part of the enlightened approach of Glenrothes' senior planning officers, who looked to Renaissance Italy as a model in their vision of integrating art into the community. During Harding's era most of the pieces, including sculptural groups, mural reliefs and pathways inscribed with poetry, were made from the same material as the townscape – raw concrete – and their position, whether in the midst of housing, on underpasses or in green areas, was always carefully chosen, though many of them have since been moved.

The 14 eclectically patterned columns that make up the stunning *Heritage* (upper photo) were created as an ironic comment on the tall, featureless office block in whose shadow they originally stood. This was art for people to live with, to sit or climb on, walk through or shelter under. Harding's successor, Malcolm Robertson, took up the torch in 1978, and in his 14-year tenure left many more landmark works, including the joyous *Giant Irises*, originally made for the 1988 Glasgow Garden Festival.

Address Photo 1: Fullerton Road, Glenrothes, KY7 5QR; photo 2: North Street, Glenrothes, KY7 5NA | Getting there An interactive map with the exact location of all of the town's 174 artworks can be found at www.fife.gov.uk/kb/docs/articles/community-life2/parks,-allotments,-core-paths. Riverside Park has a trail featuring a number of relocated 1970s hippos | Tip The volunteer-led Glenrothes and Area Heritage Centre has photographic displays and an archive of information on the history of the new town, including the Town Art programme (6–8 Marchmont Gate, Kingdom Shopping Centre, KY7 5NB).

43 Kinghorn Loch

The water that came back from the dead

With its long history as a ferry port, fishing village and scenic beach resort, the ancient burgh of Kinghorn is inextricably linked to the briny waters of the Forth estuary. Generations of holidaymakers have visited the town without realising that it also boasts a freshwater loch, just a mile inland from the shore. There is however an understandable reason for this: for much of the recent past it was a sad, lifeless place, its ecosystem poisoned by decades of pollution. Happily this has now been reversed, and the loch reborn as a wonderful community asset.

The burns that feed and flow from the loch have been a valuable resource for Kinghorn since the Middle Ages, used to power grain mills and later for industries such as barley threshing, linen making and cotton spinning. Problems began in the 1880s, when the council sued a short-lived paraffin wax factory for polluting the drinking supply. But it was in the 1950s that things got truly toxic. An aluminium works in nearby Burntisland started using a landfill site upstream to dump 'red mud' waste, an alkaline slurry that leached chemicals into the loch, creating algal bloom and extinguishing all aquatic life except midge larvae.

A decontamination programme in the early 1980s proved successful only in the short term, but in 1999 the loch became the subject of pioneering treatment (now commonplace) using rafts made of barley straw. These deter the growth of algae and clean up the water while, fortuitously, providing nesting sites for waterfowl. The loch now enjoys a rich biodiversity, and is managed primarily as a conservation site, though it's also popular with anglers, sailors and canoeists. The wooded lochside has likewise been transformed and hosts a variety of laudable enterprises, chief among them the Ecology Centre, an environmental charity that runs educational projects for all ages and abilities, and also has a welcoming café.

Address Kinghorn, Fife KY3 9YG, www.craigencalttrust.org.uk (for water sports and activities), www.theecologycentre.org.uk (for workshops and events) | Getting there Train to Kinghorn, then a 20-minute walk via Burnside Avenue and Burnside Path | Hours Unrestricted; Ecology Centre café: Mon 8.30am–2pm, Tue–Sun 9.30am–3.30pm (Tue–Thu takeaway drinks only) | Tip On the loch's north bank, look out for Art by the Loch, an open studio in Craigencalt Mill; Greenheart Growers, a social enterprise which offers organic gardening sessions (Thu 11am–4pm); and the Ecology Centre bird hide (phone +44 (0)1592 891567 for the lock combination).

44 Adam Smith Close
In the footsteps of the 'father of capitalism'

The writings of the 18th-century moral philosopher Adam Smith helped shape the modern world. One of the key figures of the Scottish Enlightenment, he is hailed as the founder of the science of economics, and his magnum opus, *The Wealth of Nations*, is said to be one of the most influential books ever written.

Smith was born in 1723 in Kirkcaldy, a community that remained the keystone of his life. Though his studies and work as an academic took him to Glasgow, Oxford, France and Edinburgh, much of the inspiration for his masterwork on how states acquire wealth came from the everyday life of his home town, where he lived quietly at his mother's house from 1767 to 1776 while completing the text. His observation of the nail makers of Pathhead led to his theories on the division of labour, while the busy waterfront where merchant ships plied to and from the Low Countries was crucial to his thinking on trade. The core ideas presented in his lengthy tome have often been misread as justifying the excesses of free market capitalism, and Smith was long ago claimed as a poster boy by the political right. But this is a crude misrepresentation of the man and the subtlety of his thinking, as is clear from his *Theory of Moral Sentiments* (1759), in which he expounds on the importance of what we would now call human empathy in underpinning a healthy economy.

Apart from giving his name to its fine civic theatre, and putting an idealised 19th-century portrait bust by Carlo Marochetti in the foyer, Kirkcaldy has been rather remiss in commemorating its greatest citizen. A little plaque marks the site of the long-gone family house; next door, a narrow, 328-foot passageway where Smith would have walked down to the sea has been belatedly renamed and paved with slabs inscribed to mark key events in his life. At the far end of the close is a visitor centre established by a local foundation committed to celebrating his legacy, though this is not yet regularly open.

Address Between 222 and 224 High Street, Kirkcaldy, KY1 1JT | **Getting there** Train to Kirkcaldy or bus to Kirkcaldy Bus Station; the entrance to the close is just to the right of the pet shop | **Hours** See www.adamsmithglobalfoundation.com for information on visitor centre | **Tip** Two minutes' walk away in historic Kirk Wynd is Kirkcaldy Old Kirk, the former parish church where Smith was baptised. With a sturdy 15th-century tower and fine stained glass designed by Burne-Jones, it's being developed as a heritage centre, and is currently a venue for concerts and events (www.kirkcaldyoldkirktrust.org.uk).

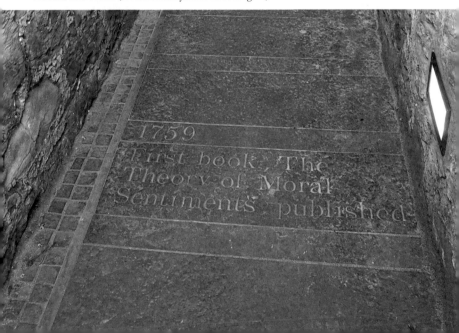

45 The Art Gallery
A brush with Scottish colour

The long building that flanks the pleasant gardens next to Kirkcaldy Station has a plain, sombre exterior that seems to belie its agreeable function as a temple of art and culture. Such sobriety is, however, in keeping with the mood of the times in which it was built, and the dual purpose it was intended to fulfil, for Kirkcaldy's art gallery and museum, which opened in 1925, was designed as an integral part of the town's memorial to the dead of World War I. The land was donated and the construction costs funded by local linoleum magnate John Nairn in memory of his only son Ian, who had been killed in action just two months before the Armistice. Nairn also gifted paintings to the gallery's founding collection; this later grew to be of national significance, with many works by leading members of the two bright, bold and radical collectives known as the Glasgow Boys and the Scottish Colourists.

Kirkcaldy's civic art museum arrived rather late on the UK scene (although it might not have existed at all had it not been for Nairn's personal tragedy). The movement to give the British public free access to fine art had begun a century earlier, with the opening in 1824 of London's National Gallery, whose core collection was bequeathed by businessman John Julius Angerstein. This set the tone for the 19th-century boom in provincial galleries filled with art contributed by local industrialists. In Kirkcaldy's case it was John W. Blyth, a linen manufacturer and avid collector of Scottish painting, who as honorary curator provided the jewels in the crown of the town's art – the joyous still lifes of S.J. Peploe and haunting impressionistic seascapes of William McTaggart. In recent years the gallery has acquired several paintings by self-taught Fifer Jack Vettriano, whose chilly Leven Beach fantasy *The Singing Butler* must be the most reproduced image in all Scottish art. There is also plenty to appeal to younger visitors, with activities, art materials and sources of inspiration all on hand.

Address Kirkcaldy Galleries, War Memorial Gardens, Kirkcaldy, KY1 1YG, +44 (0)1592 583206, www.onfife.com/venues/kirkcaldy-galleries | Getting there Train to Kirkcaldy or bus to Kirkcaldy Bus Station | Hours Daily, times vary; check website for current information | Tip Just across the road is the Adam Smith Theatre, where the admirable Fife Opera stage their annual productions. This fine, largely amateur company (one of the few remaining in Scotland devoted to grand opera) has members of all ages, and is particularly committed to nurturing young singers.

46__The Coptic Screen
Linktown's link to Egypt

It's quite a journey from the deserts of Egypt in biblical times to the waterfront of Kirkcaldy at the end of the second millennium. Yet it was in a humdrum setting a stone's throw from the Links Sands that the Coptic Orthodox Church chose to establish its first place of worship in Scotland, around 1,950 years after their beginnings in the city of Alexandria. Traditionally believed to have been founded by St Mark, author of the second New Testament gospel, the Church of the Copts (whose name comes from the Greek term for Egypt) is one of the earliest Christian faiths.

The plain, gabled, mid 19th-century façade, of what was originally Invertiel Free Church, gives no hint of the transformation of the interior, now deftly remodelled to meet the requirements of orthodox worship. There is a profusion of intricately carved woodwork, with pews and other furniture repeatedly emblazoned with the distinctive motif of the Coptic cross.

But it is the magnificent iconostasis, the vast screen filled with holy images which separates the main body of the church from the inner sanctuary, that immediately commands attention. A gift from Pope Shenouda III, who consecrated the church in 1992, it includes 10,000 elements, all carved, gilded and painted in Egypt, then shipped to Kirkcaldy and assembled on-site by Coptic craftsmen. On the curtain screening the archway to the sanctuary is St Mark, with evangelical pen in hand and accompanied by his symbolic lion; rather less familiar to visitors is the figure of St Menas, an Egyptian soldier turned hermit who became a willing martyr at an early age, and is popularly depicted with two supportive camels.

The church serves a congregation of at least 15 nationalities, many of whom travel from far-flung parts of Scotland and northern England to worship at the Sunday services, which are conducted in Arabic and English and are open to all.

Address St Mark's Coptic Orthodox Church, 251 Links Street, Kirkcaldy, KY1 1QE, +44 (0)7817 771535, www.stmarkcopticscotland.org | **Getting there** Train to Kirkcaldy and a 20-minute walk; bus 7 to Links Street | **Hours** Sun 10am–3pm | **Tip** On a brick gable end just across the street is a large, intriguing mural in perforated steel by Andy Scott (sculptor of Falkirk's famous *Kelpies*) celebrating several inspiring aspects of Kirkcaldy's history, including the invention of global time zones by native son Sir Sandford Fleming.

47 _ Dysart

From a legendary saint to a fictional outlander

A trail round the characterful byways of Dysart involves quite a few ups and downs, rather appropriately for a town that has seen some marked changes of fortune over the centuries. Its name derives from a complex of caves used in ancient times as a retreat – *deserta* in Latin – allegedly by St Serf, the much-mythologised figure who brought Christianity to Fife in the 6th century. This is now in the grounds of a Carmelite convent, near the commanding 72-foot tower of the old church dedicated to the saint, built around 1500. By that time, Dysart was an established centre for the manufacture and export of salt, produced by boiling sea water in huge iron pans fired by coal, a dirty and laborious business carried out along the level ground by the shore. Known as Pan Ha', this is today a tranquil green sward fringed with picturesque 16th- and 17th-century workers' housing, rescued from dereliction in the 1960s and restored to immaculate quaintness (see ch. 109).

Trade continued for centuries with the Low Countries and the Baltic states in coal, fish, beer and linen as well as salt. Demand for this hard-won commodity fluctuated according to the political situation on the continent, with booms at times when the purer French 'bay salt' was unobtainable. By the 19th century, coal mining was Dysart's dominant industry, and the harbour was enlarged to cope with the volume of trade, incorporating the wall of a former quarry hewn out of the cliffside.

Still overlooking today's very much quieter maritime scene is the four-square Harbourmaster's House, now renovated as the headquarters of the Fife Coast and Countryside Trust. In 2015, the attractive quayside became a CGI-enhanced location for the *Outlander* TV series, standing in for the port of Le Havre in the 1740s, where time-travelling heroine Claire and her Highland lad Jamie land when they escape to France.

Address Dysart, Kirkcaldy, KY1 2TQ | Getting there Bus X60 or X61 to West Quality Street and walk down Hot Pot Wynd, or alight at Ravenscraig Park and follow the coastal path east to Dysart Harbour | Tip At the top of the town, Dysart St Clair Church houses an unexpected treasure: stunning murals by the great Charles Rennie Mackintosh, painted in 1902, later covered up and only recently rediscovered and restored (www.dysartstclair.org.uk). There is also a highly original gravestone by Mackintosh in the Macduff Cemetery at East Wemyss, 4 miles up the coast.

48__Fife Ice Arena

Get your skates on

Kirkcaldy Ice Rink caused a sensation when it opened its doors on 1 October, 1938. There were traffic jams for miles around as an eager public and invited dignitaries flocked to the state-of-the-art stadium to enjoy a day-long spectacle, including a curling tournament and figure skating displays, and culminating in the debut of the town's fledgling ice hockey team, the Fife Flyers. Like many others in the UK, the Kirkcaldy squad was born out of a massive craze for the game triggered by the momentous gold medal win of the British ice hockey team at the 1936 Winter Olympics.

It was predicted that in Scotland the sport could grow to rival football in popularity, until the outbreak of war put paid to plans for constructing a score of new rinks. The Flyers are the sole survivors of that boom time. The longest-established professional team in the UK, they're still based at the same venue, now renamed Fife Ice Arena, and currently play in the Elite Ice Hockey League, followed by their exuberant and vocal fans. Generations of Fifers have become knowledgeable and critical spectators of the fast-paced, physical sport. Skating on blades just half a millimetre thick, players can reach speeds of 20 miles per hour, and the atmosphere is electric as they dodge and race across the ice pad in pursuit of the all-important puck.

As the oldest operational rink in Scotland, offering skating sessions, curling classes and more besides, the building is itself a remarkable survival. Designed by local architects Williamson and Hubbard to house 4,000 spectators, its final cost was a tidy £40,000. The arena, whose unsupported roof span of 145 feet was the widest in the country at the time of its construction, has seen some necessary modernisation, but the glamorously streamlined entrance bay in classic Art Deco style remains virtually unaltered. Other features of the original high-end decor included Parker Knoll furniture and fabrics designed by Dame Laura Knight, all sadly long gone.

Address Rosslyn Street, Kirkcaldy, KY1 3HS, +44 (0)1592 595100 | **Getting there** Bus X37 | Hours Daily; see website for times of skating sessions and classes, and fifeflyers.co.uk for hockey fixtures | **Tip** Kirkcaldy's other major sporting venue is Stark's Park football stadium, home of Raith Rovers F.C. Local authors Ian Rankin and Val McDermid are among the celebrity fans of the team immortalised in the 1960s by the unwitting gaffe uttered by BBC commentator Sam Leitch after one of their victories, '...and they'll be dancing in the streets of Raith tonight!'

49 The Linoleum Poem
The magical mixture with the 'queer-like smell'

The waiting area on Platform 1 at Kirkcaldy station is a bleak 1980s 'architectural statement' that provides little comfort for the weary traveller. But it does have one unique saving grace. Emblazoned on the wall is a poetic tribute to the golden days of rail travel, that includes a cheeky allusion to the local product in which its very words are inlaid – linoleum.

'The Boy in the Train' was written in 1913 for the magazine of Merchiston School in Edinburgh by Mary Campbell Smith, the headmaster's wife, who was inspired by a garrulous wee lad she overheard while travelling to Elie for a family holiday. Some of the dialect terms may puzzle non-Scots, but the gist of his breathless commentary is surely clear (despite the contrived 'Kirkcaddy' – easier to rhyme than the correct pronunciation, KirCAWdy). After the sounds, sights and tastes of the journey comes the smell: the last couplet evokes the unmistakable odour that used to pervade the town due to the process of manufacturing 'lino' flooring, which at its height occupied seven huge factories that exported all over the world and put Kirkcaldy on the map.

For its makers, there is poetry of a different kind in the complex alchemy by which oxidised linseed oil, wood flour, cork dust, pine rosin and pigments meld together to form the magical cement which is then pressed on to a hessian backing. The ingredients and processes haven't really changed since 1863, when its inventor, Frederick Walton, applied for a patent – but failed to register the name 'linoleum' as a trademark. Kirkcaldy entrepreneur Michael Nairn quickly saw its potential, and his legacy brought a century of prosperity to the town. Though it fell out of favour with the introduction of vinyl flooring in the 1980s, linoleum is now enjoying a quiet comeback, the fruits of an image makeover, aided in part by its impeccably green credentials as a sustainable natural product.

THE BOY IN THE TRAIN

Whit wey does the engine say Toot-toot?
  Is it feart to gang in the tunnel?
Whit wey is the furnace no pit oot?
  When the rain gangs doon the funnel?
What'll I hae for my tea the nicht?
  A herrin', or maybe a haddie?
Has Gran'ma gotten electric licht?
  Is the next stop Kirkcaddy?

There's a hoodie-craw on yon turnip-raw!
  An' sea gulls! - sax or seeven.
I'll no fa'oot o' the windae, Maw,
  It's sneckit, as sure as I'm leevin'.
We're into the tunnel! we're a' in the dark!
  But dinna be frichtit, Daddy,
We'll sune be comin' to Beveridge Park,
  And the next stop's Kirkcaddy!

Is yon the mune I see in the sky?
  It's awfu' wee an' curly.
See! there's a coo and a cauf ootbye,
  An' a lassie pu'in' a hurly!
He's chackit the tickets and gien them back,
  Sae gie me my ain yin, Daddy,
Lift doon the bag frae the luggage rack,
  For the next stop's Kirkcaddy!

There's a gey wheen boats at the harbour mou',
  And eh! dae ye see the cruisers?
The cinnamon drop I was sookin' the noo
  Has tummelt an' stuck tae ma troosers....
I'll sune be ringin' ma Gran'ma's bell,
  She'll cry, "Come ben, my laddie."
For I ken mysel' by the queer - like smell
  That the next stop's Kirkcaddy!

(MARY CAMPBELL SMITH)

Michael Nairn began making floorcloth in Kirkcaldy in 1847 and in 1878 began the manufacture of the linoleum for which the town and its sweet smell became famous. Today linoleum is again in demand world-wide. The Forbo-Nairn factory, also well-known for its Cushionflor, is the only linoleum plant in Britain.

Cut in Linoleum

Address Kirkcaldy Station, off Abbotshall Road, Kirkcaldy, KY1 1YL | Getting there Train to Kirkcaldy (obviously) or bus to Railway Station | Hours Open daily | Tip Kirkcaldy Galleries, right next door to the station, have an excellent display on floorcloth and linoleum, including tools that will be familiar to those who remember the childhood pleasure of making linocuts (www.onfife.com/venues/kirkcaldy-galleries). The Forbo Flooring factory, the only remaining linoleum manufacturer in the UK, is at Den Road, Kirkcaldy, KY1 2ER (www.forbo.com; not open to the public).

50 Maggie's Centre
A whole new angle on a challenging issue

The only conventional aspect of Maggie's Fife cancer care centre is the NHS sign indicating the path leading to it, in the grounds of Kirkcaldy's Victoria Hospital. With its sharp angles and curious little windows, the exterior of the low black building looks frankly forbidding. Turning its back on the anonymous multi-storey blocks, Maggie's faces instead into a wooded hollow, while its dark, pointed shell, folded like a giant piece of origami, protectively envelops a long, glass entrance wall. But as soon as you cross the threshold, the building seems to open up, Tardis-like, in a quite unexpected way, and you find yourself in a warm, comfortable environment, with a series of light-filled, organic spaces, centred on a kitchen where the kettle is always on. First-time visitors are taken aback by the domesticity of the place, the welcoming staff and atmosphere of relaxed informality, even light-heartedness.

Maggie's Centres exist to complement the clinical work of hospitals, offering free professional advice and support of all kinds to cancer patients and their loved ones. The idea took shape in the mind of designer Maggie Keswick Jencks after a 1993 diagnosis giving her only months to live left her struggling to process the news in the bleak, windowless corridor of an Edinburgh hospital. In the event, she had two years to develop her life-enhancing concept; the plans for the first centre were on her bed when she died.

Her husband, the architectural theorist and artist Charles Jencks (see ch. 21) saw that project and subsequent ones to fruition, with the help of some talented friends, and there are now 30 Maggie's Centres in the UK and beyond, all of them architecturally innovative, with the majority designed by famous names. Maggie's Fife was the fifth; opened in 2006, it was the first built work in the UK by Zaha Hadid, then the world's most celebrated female architect. In 2019, its busiest year to date, the centre had over 8,600 visits.

Address Victoria Hospital, Hayfield Road, Kirkcaldy, KY2 5AH, +44 (0)1592 647997, www.maggies.org | **Getting there** Bus from Kirkcaldy Bus Station to Victoria Hospital; Maggie's is opposite the main entrance | **Hours** Drop-in for cancer patients and relatives, Mon–Fri 9am–5pm; otherwise viewable from exterior | **Tip** Back in the town centre, the highly-rated Roots and Seeds Café Bistro at 73 High Street offers wholesome, freshly cooked fare including tasty Latin-American options (+44 (0)1592 266182, Mon–Sat 8.30am–5pm, plus tapas evenings in summer).

51 The Merchant's House

A grand design and a ghost ship

With a main thoroughfare that now extends for four miles, it's easy to see why Kirkcaldy has adopted the nickname 'the Lang Toun' (long town). More difficult to appreciate today is the original focus of this highway – the port that grew up in the Middle Ages around a sheltered cove, which by the end of the 17th century had become one of the busiest harbours in Scotland.

In his guide book to Britain published in the 1720s, Daniel Defoe waxes lyrical about Kirkcaldy's 'considerable' merchants and their 'several good ships', the 'very well built' town and its flourishing export trade. The harbour is now a much more modest sight, but a glimpse of its glory days can be found in the waterfront Merchant's House, a rare survival dating from about 1590.

The prestigious three-storey house was built for merchant and shipowner David Law, and later passed into the hands of other rich local families. But by the early 19th century the area was no longer a desirable residential neighbourhood, and the building was subdivided into flats and commercial premises. It was in serious disrepair in the mid-1980s when the newly formed Scottish Historic Buildings Trust took it on as their first conservation project. They were delighted to discover how much interior decoration from the 16th and 17th centuries had survived under the later overlay – painted beams with stylised flower and fruit designs, elaborate decorative plasterwork and geometrically patterned panels. The most exceptional find was a ghostly mural fragment of a 16th-century galleon in full sail; it's thought that this could depict the vessel in which James VI's new queen, Anne of Denmark, made a royal progress round the Forth ports in 1590. Another notable survival is the long strip of land, or rig, at the back of the house, originally used for growing crops and keeping animals, and now restored as a community garden. It can be accessed from the popular courtyard café which occupies part of the ground floor.

Address Law's Close, 339–343 High Street, Kirkcaldy, KY1 1JL, www.facebook.com/LawsClose | Getting there Train to Kirkcaldy or bus to Kirkcaldy Bus Station | Hours Variable: the house is let out to shops and small businesses. Merchant's House Café: Wed–Mon 9am–5pm | Tip The Duchess of Kirkcaldy is a retro-themed bar and music venue at the other end of the High Street. Its name comes from the Beatles' song 'Cry Baby Cry' and recalls the nickname John Lennon gave to Mary Yardley, the agent who booked the Fab Four for their legendary Kirkcaldy gig on 9 October, 1963 at the now demolished Carlton Cinema.

52 — 'Pet Marjorie'
The reinvention of a feisty wunderkind

In the summer of 1808, a precociously bright six-year-old called Marjory Fleming was sent from her native Kirkcaldy to stay with relatives in Edinburgh. There she was tutored by her cousin Isabella, who encouraged her eager but wilful pupil to keep a diary. Marjory took to this task with relish, filling three journals with stream-of-consciousness accounts of her impressions of the world. Vividly enhanced by her remarkable vocabulary and cheerfully erratic spelling, these veer seamlessly from comical to poignant as she expresses her delight in nature and animals, comments on religion and public hangings, gives pithy character sketches of ladies and 'bucks', and chastises herself for her own temper tantrums. Her poetry, on themes ranging from a charming pet monkey to a scandalous elopement, was clearly harder work, and she is irresistibly funny about the difficulty of finding rhymes. But Marjory's burgeoning creative life was sadly cut short when, four weeks before her ninth birthday, she died of meningitis.

It was not till 1930 that her grave monument was erected. The sculptor, Pilkington Jackson, was more at home creating grandiose memorials to heroic men, and his meek, saintly figure is an insipid tribute to Marjory's exuberant free spirit. But by then she had achieved huge posthumous fame internationally as 'Pet Marjorie', the embodiment of guileless childhood innocence. This all began in 1847 with an article in the *Fife Herald*, which gave a sentimentalised, bowdlerised version of her life and output (removing words like 'bottom' and 'bitch'), and continued with her later fictitious reinvention as the bonnie wee muse of Walter Scott. (She had a distant family connection to the great author, but there is no evidence that they ever met.) Had she lived, Marjory might well have become a novelist, conceivably – given her evident interest in both Gothic thrillers and real-life murders – an early precursor of Kirkcaldy's own Val McDermid, in the genre of mystery and suspense.

Address Abbotshall Kirkyard, Abbotshall Road, Kirkcaldy, KY2 5PH | **Getting there** Train to Kirkcaldy or bus to Kirkcaldy Bus Station; the grave is near the south-west corner of the churchyard | **Hours** Unrestricted | **Tip** Marjory's journals are in the collections of the National Library of Scotland; they can be viewed in facsimile, together with a haunting miniature portrait of her, at www.digital.nls.uk. Also available online are recordings of the songs *A Garland for Marjory Fleming*, Richard Rodney Bennett's delightful 1969 setting of five of her sonnets.

53 The Bull Stone

The gory past of a peaceful green

At the east end of the town of Leslie is its ancient village green, once the hub of the community but now a quiet residential corner, with even the former parish church converted into flats. Planted solidly near the northern edge of the grassy sward is a curiously shaped granite boulder, three feet high, that to some eyes has the appearance of modern sculpture – perhaps an unfinished portrait bust by some follower of Henry Moore. But the Bull Stone, as it's known, hides a longer and much darker history.

The deep grooves around the middle are the result of centuries of wear from the ropes and chains used to secure bulls for the hideous practice of bull-baiting. This 'sport' took various forms, sometimes using a pit, but basically involved setting specially bred dogs, one by one, on a bull tethered firmly by the leg or neck. (Bears would be substituted on special occasions.) The attack dogs, bred for aggression, were trained to go for the animal's nose, which had often been blown full of pepper to annoy it. A dog that succeeded in fastening its teeth securely to the snout was said to have 'pinned the bull'; others would be gored or tossed in the air. The bloody spectacle would go on for hours, in front of a baying crowd of all ages and social classes; it was actually believed that this torment improved the quality of the bull's meat.

The prevalence of this barbaric pastime, widespread across Britain from early medieval times, must give us pause for thought about what was considered family entertainment by former generations. Though banned by the Puritans in 1642 during the Civil War, it continued after the Restoration in 1660, and in fact it wasn't till 1835 that it was finally outlawed, along with other blood sports, by Act of Parliament. A prior attempt in 1800 to abolish the practice had failed after a fierce debate, during which future prime minister George Canning described it as an 'amusement', declaring 'What could be more innocent than bull-baiting, boxing or dancing?'

Address Greenside, Leslie, KY6 3DF | **Getting there** Bus 39A/C to Leslie High Street (Greenside Hotel); the stone is on the far side of the green | **Tip** The imposing entrance in the wall opposite the green leads into the wooded grounds of Leslie House, ancestral seat of the Rothes family, described by Daniel Defoe in the 1720s as 'the glory … of the whole province of Fife'. Reconstructed after burning down in 1763, the building was again badly damaged by fire in 2009. In 2021, work began to restore the derelict shell as part of a housing development, in what local councillors described as the 'least worst option' for the site.

54_Fife Heritage Railway

Hear that whistle blowing

Steam trains fascinate like no other mode of transport. In our sanitised modern world, where engines and the energy that drives them are discreetly hidden away, the mere sight of one of these puffing, clanking, hissing, ruggedly magnificent workhorses evokes exhilaration and delight in young and old alike. Now, thanks to years of sterling effort by the Kingdom of Fife Railway Preservation Society, visitors to the former Kirkland marshalling yard can get a genuine taste of the great age of steam. On select Sundays, the society offers brief but memorably nostalgic trips along their half-mile track, pulled by the painstakingly restored *Forth*, a sturdy saddle-tank locomotive built in 1926 at the Andrew Barclay works in Kilmarnock.

Rather more *Thomas the Tank Engine* than *Flying Scotsman* (which only adds to her general appeal), *Forth* spent most of her working life at Granton Gas Works in Edinburgh, and was brought to Fife in the 1980s by the now-defunct Lochty Private Railway. Since her acquisition for Fife Heritage Railway, she has been repainted in the historic livery of the Wemyss Coal Company, to match sister locomotives of fond local memory. The coach she draws dates from 1914 and originally ran on Norwegian State Railways; volunteers worked for many months on its restoration and immaculate retro-fitting, after researching its varied history. This is proudly illustrated on the information panels which you can peruse on your short journey.

Open day visitors can also experience the thrill of being a 'driver for a fiver', taking control of the versatile *River Eden*, a diesel engine built in 1955 by the North British Locomotive Company and formerly in use as a shunter at RAF Leuchars. There are further restoration projects ongoing in the engine shed, including two undeniably cute little locomotives affectionately known as the Dubbie Pug and the Burntisland Barclay. Society members are happy to discuss their work, and new volunteers are always welcome.

Address Kirkland Railway Yard, Burnmill Industrial Estate, Leven, KY8 4RB, www.fifeheritagerailway.co.uk | **Getting there** Bus 7, X60 or X61 to Leven Bus Station | **Hours** Running days: Apr–Oct, last Sun of the month 11am–4pm, plus pre-Christmas specials. Site open all year Tue & Sat 11am–5pm (though no trains run then) | **Tip** Methil Heritage Centre is a small, lovingly run community museum devoted to the history of the area known officially as Levenmouth. It's housed in the old post office, which was built in 1936 and boasts a rare carved stone cipher of King Edward VIII (272 High Street, Methil, KY8 3EQ, Tue–Thu 11.30am–4.30pm, Sat 1–4pm).

55 Dalginch

The gathering place at Fife's ancient heart

Nestling in the arc of a burn at the north-eastern limit of Markinch is a steeply sloping swathe of grass dotted with overgrown topiary, the site since 1853 of Northall Cemetery. The shady avenues of yew trees and irregular scattering of weathered headstones create a haunting impression that even the nearby railway line can't dispel – not spooky or melancholy, as you might expect of a Victorian burial ground, but distinctly unworldly nonetheless. Both local historians and enthusiasts of 19th-century sculpture will appreciate its monuments, which include a superb Celtic cross from 1884 by architect and designer Sydney Mitchell, commemorating Robert F. Balfour of Balbirnie, and a white marble slab carved with a delicate palm tree motif in memory of William Tullis and Agnes Russell, whose marriage sealed the future of the papermaking firm that was a major presence in the town for generations.

The cemetery was only in use until 1900, but in a more distant era the land that houses it had enormous significance for the whole region. This simple mound of earth is in fact an early medieval moot hill – an open-air gathering place where judicial business was settled, disputes resolved and proclamations made. The ancient terraces on nearby Markinch Hill probably served as viewing platforms for the local populace. Moot hills are found throughout north-west Europe, and were generally built to order, often by modifying sacred prehistoric sites. Northall used to be known as Prickhilly, which seems thematically linked to its more ancient name of Dalginch – Gaelic for 'isle of thorns'. In the 12th century, Dalginch was described as one of the seven chief places of justice in Scotland; it seems likely that it was chosen for that role in Pictish times because of its central – and neutral – location, on the border between the sub-kingdoms of Fothriff to the south-west and Fife to the north-east. Presumably they got rid of the thorny plants before they got down to the thorny problems.

Address Northall Cemetery, Northall Road, Markinch, KY7 6JR | **Getting there** Train to Markinch | **Hours** Unrestricted | **Tip** The dedicated members of Markinch Heritage Group have done a great deal to interpret the historic sights of this fascinating town. A leaflet is available outlining the Braes Loan trail, and there are information boards at sites including Markinch Hill, with its mysterious ancient terraces, and the parish church, whose stunning Romanesque tower is one of the finest in Scotland (www.markinchheritage.org.uk).

56 Alexander III Monument
It was a dark and stormy night …

On 19 March, 1286, the steep embankment above Pettycur Bay was the site of the most momentous tragedy in early Scottish history: the death of the last of Scotland's Celtic kings, Alexander III. Earlier that day he had attended a council at Edinburgh Castle, followed by a feast to celebrate his recent marriage (the 44-year-old had been a widower for a decade). He declared his intention to travel that very night to his manor at Kinghorn, where his young French wife Yolande was waiting. The weather was foul by the time his ferry reached the Fife shore, but Alexander ignored advice and rode on through the dark. He was nearing his destination along the clifftop road when his attendants lost sight of him in the storm; his body was found the next morning on rocks above the beach, near that of his horse.

Alexander's sudden, untimely death marked the end of a period of peace and prosperity that later came to be known as Scotland's Golden Age. He had no living offspring to take his place; Yolande was already pregnant, but the child was stillborn. The complex crisis of succession that followed led to a long, bloody conflict with England, and general bad feeling between the two nations that many would say has never really gone away.

The memorial cross erected in 1887 on the stone where the king's body was found is now awkwardly accommodated in a narrow layby on the A 921. Traffic roars by at your side, trains chunter along the coastal line below and static holiday caravans teeter high overhead on the fateful clifftop as you muse on these distant events.

Alexander's sexual appetite was legendary: according to one medieval chronicler, '…he would visit, none too creditably, nuns or matrons, virgins or widows, as the fancy seized him, sometimes in disguise'. If only he had been content to dally with an Edinburgh lass on that dark and stormy night, the course of Scottish history might have been utterly different.

Address Kingswoodend, Kinghorn Road, KY3 9LL | Getting there On A 921 to west of Kinghorn – parking in layby; bus 7 or X57 to Kinghorn Road (Kingswood Hotel) | Tip Scotland's Golden Age may be long gone, but the golden sands of Pettycur Bay, just below Alexander's monument, are still there for all to enjoy. The vast expanse of beach, with wonderful views across the water to Edinburgh and the Lothians, is best accessed from the town of Kinghorn, a short way to the east.

57 Auld Wemyss Ways

The chattering parrot and the sentinel canary

It's astonishing how rapidly the deindustrialisation process removed virtually all trace of the collieries that were a major feature of Fife's landscape until the 1980s. Much of the material evidence of the miners' everyday lives has likewise been discarded, a regrettable outcome that is now being addressed by the remarkable Auld Wemyss Ways. Opened in 2013, the volunteer-run heritage centre occupies a converted bunkhouse, formerly used by walkers on the Fife Coastal Path.

It's difficult to resist using journalistic clichés for this tiny hidden gem, tucked up a wynd in the out-of-the-way village of West Wemyss. Step across its portals and another well-worn phrase leaps to mind: treasure trove. If you're sceptical about how a collection of coal mining memorabilia could merit such a glowing tag, a tour of its two jam-packed rooms will soon put you right. What it lacks in labels is made up for by its dedicated and enthusiastic staff of one, Tom Moffet, curator and veritable (ahem) mine of information.

One surprise is the quantity of deeply felt art on display: haunting images by self-taught ex-miner George Beckwith, who painted all the local collieries (except, on principle, the controversial Rothes Pit) and an evocative watercolour of the Michael Colliery (which closed in 1967 after a horrific fire) by Duncan Gilfillan, former mine surveyor and champion of mining heritage. Below it is a tray of bricks more intriguing and genuinely meaningful than any conceptual artwork, recalling the important industry that depended on the pits' discarded shale. There are intricate carvings of miners at work, made out of parrot coal (so-called because of the chattering noise it made when burned), and a cage cover for a canary, kept to detect toxic gases – the paradigm of what scientists call a sentinel species. It's painted with a sensitivity worthy of Craigie Aitchison, the Fife-born Royal Academician whose whimsical canvases often featured a similarly touching little yellow bird.

Address 1 Narrow Wynd, West Wemyss, KY1 4SZ, +44 (0)1592 599044, www.facebook.com/auldwemyssways | Getting there Bus 7/7A to Coaltown of Wemyss (West Wemyss Toll) and a 15-minute walk | Hours Fri–Sun noon–3pm or by arrangement; contact ziggymoffet@hotmail.co.uk | Tip West Wemyss is a planned village, built for workers on the Wemyss Estate around the old harbour, a thriving coal port in the 19th century. In the vestry of the parish church is a gravestone carved out of parrot coal by talented mason Thomas Williamson, whose ornate coal furniture can be seen in Kirkcaldy Galleries.

58__ The Fisheries Museum
Farlans, Zulus and the real price of fish

Few visitors to Anstruther can resist the draw of its most popular attraction – fish and chips from the much-vaunted Fish Bar on Shore Street, preferably consumed on a bench overlooking the harbour. But anyone seeking an in-depth appreciation of just what it takes to deliver their hallowed haddock to the quayside should also spend time exploring the outstanding institution just along the road. The 18 varied and fascinating galleries of the Scottish Fisheries Museum give a truly humbling insight into the harvesting of the sea, as they unfold the histories of the 'boats, fish and folk' involved in this perennially challenging industry.

The museum opened over 50 years ago, just as the North Sea herring shoals that once sustained a vast local fishing fleet were beginning to decline dramatically. Its home, a motley group of old buildings known as St Ayles, has fishing connections dating back to 1318; its territory has, however, expanded over the years, and the museum's modest street frontage now belies its true scale. Ranked as nationally significant, its collections comprise over 65,000 items related to the Scottish fishing industry past and present, everything from historic photographs, costume and paintings to fishing equipment, boat models – and 22 full-sized vessels, including the flagship *Reaper*, a handsome 70-foot 'Fifie' herring drifter built in 1901. She has graced films and TV series both factual and fictional, including Outlander.

Allow an hour or two for your visit: you will find much food for thought. The re-creation of a herring market gives a vivid picture of the 'farlans', where women used to gut an incredible 60 fish per minute. You can sit at the helm in an original wheelhouse, step inside a traditional fisherman's cottage, and see the scale of the mighty Zulu fishing boats, named in 1879 out of sympathy with the South African warriors. Most poignant of all is the memorial room dedicated to Scottish fishermen lost at sea.

Address Harbourhead, Anstruther, KY10 3AB, +44 (0)1333 310628, www.scotfishmuseum.org | Getting there Bus 95 or X60 to Anstruther (Fisheries Museum) | Hours Apr–Sept, Mon–Sat 10am–5.30pm, Sun 11am–5pm; Oct–Mar, Mon–Sat 10am–4.30pm, Sun noon–4.30pm | Tip A novel way to begin a tour of this captivating town is by following the model of the solar system, scaled down to one ten-thousand-millionth of its size, on a series of 11 bronze plates. They're fixed to walls along Shore Street and beyond, with Earth and its nearest neighbours on the Fisheries Museum frontage; walk to the Anstruther Fish Bar and you'll have reached Jupiter.

59___The Isle of May
Where the sky meets the sea

Seen from afar, the island that locals simply call 'the May' can exert a mysterious fascination. It's a shape-shifter, undergoing continual changes in appearance according to your viewpoint along the East Neuk coast, as well as the vagaries of the weather and the light. But for truly immersive enchantment, a trip to its rocky shores, out in the widest reaches of the Firth of Forth, is a must.

The May boasts a long and intriguing heritage: one of Scotland's earliest Christian sites, it attracted monks and pilgrims for 1,000 years to the priory and healing shrine of St Ethernan. The devout King David I founded a monastery here around 1145; part of the monks' ten-seater communal toilet survives in the ruins. In 1636 the isle's lighthouse, the first in Scotland, lent it a new significance. Originally capped with a coal-fired beacon, this was left as a romantic ruin when its grand replacement was built in 1816. Today, however, the island's human history is eclipsed by its outstanding importance as a nature reserve. Only a mile long, it teems with a spectacular wealth of wild-life: at the height of the breeding season an astonishing 200,000 sea-birds nest on its terraced cliffs and bumpy grassland – guillemots, razorbills, kittiwakes, fulmars, shags, eider ducks, terns and puffins. A variety of migrant birds make stopovers – some 285 species have been recorded, lately including the gorgeous bluethroat – and it also supports one of the country's largest grey seal nurseries.

For many visitors, the busy puffin colony is the May's star attraction. Every spring over 40,000 pairs of these hardy little seabirds return to their nest burrows for four months, resuming their lifelong bond and producing a single chick, or puffling. Parents share rearing responsi-bilities, carrying clutches of expertly fished sandeels in their powerful rainbow beaks. Equally unmistakable are the defensive Arctic terns, superlative flyers who complete an annual 22,000-mile round trip on their extraordinary migratory journeys.

Address Access by ferry from Middle Pier, Anstruther, KY10 3AB | Getting there Bus 95 or X60 to Anstruther (Fisheries Museum), then via the *May Princess* (www.isleofmayferry.com) or *Osprey* (www.isleofmayboattrips.co.uk) | Hours Apr–Sept, daily sailings, times vary. The *May Princess* trip usually allows up to three hours ashore | Tip More wildlife – gannets on the wing, dolphins and even whales – can be spotted from the boat. In July, the return trip often features a close look at a fledgling puffin: disoriented pufflings rescued by nature reserve staff are given to the crew for release in the open sea.

60 Kellie Castle

Reviving the sleeping beauty of the East Neuk

The story of this splendid tower-house-cum-mansion goes back almost seven centuries. Past residents range from a daughter of Robert the Bruce to one of the finest British composers of the 18th century, the rakish Thomas Erskine, though it's now most celebrated for the later occupants who rescued it from dereliction, turning an abandoned castle into a welcoming family home. The protagonists of this classic fantasy scenario are, however, not the ostentatious super-rich, nor an over-zealous 'improving' architect, but a unique artistic dynasty: the Lorimers.

It was in 1878 that the lease of the empty and overgrown Kellie was granted to Edinburgh law professor James Lorimer, for use as a holiday house. An Elie architect, John Currie, was appointed to supervise repairs, informed by Lorimer's own research; everything, including the restoration of exquisite 17th-century plasterwork, was carried out with painstaking respect for historical integrity. Lorimer's teenage son Robert was involved from the start, gaining hands-on skills from local craftsmen; he went on to become a prolific architect and promoter of the Arts and Crafts Movement. His elder brother John, a fine painter who often used Kellie for his inspiration, set up his studio in a tower overlooking the traditional walled garden, which was itself sensitively re-established thanks to Robert and his sister Louise. It was John who commissioned one of the castle's most surprising treasures: the Botticellian mural *Cupid's Darts*, painted in 1897 by the estimable Phoebe Traquair.

A new phase in Kellie's fortunes began in 1937 when Robert's son Hew, a distinguished sculptor best known for his large-scale work, took over the tenancy with his wife Mary; together they put their own stamp on the interior, creating an all-white look embellished with curtains and embroideries. Since Mary's death in 1970 the castle has been cared for by the National Trust for Scotland.

Address Arncroach, Pittenweem, KY10 2RF, +44 (0)1333 720271, www.nts.org.uk | Getting there Off B 9171, just east of Arncroach village; for Fife Council's bookable Go-Flexi taxibus service see www.fife.gov.uk | Hours Apr–Oct, daily 11am–5pm (Tue–Thu guided tours only); estate open all year, Thu–Mon, dawn–dusk | Tip Four miles south, the ruins of Newark Castle stand on the cliffs just west of St Monans. In the 1890s Robert Lorimer drew up plans, never executed, for its restoration and extension as a grand residence. His client was Glasgow shipping magnate and art collector Sir William Burrell.

61 Cellardyke Harbour
The silvery scales of Skinfast

With its sandy beach, popular eateries and busy harbour, the Anstruther waterfront attracts crowds of appreciative visitors throughout the season, and it's a delightful place to while away a sunny day. But for those who prefer to unwind by just sitting on a dockside 'watchin' the tide roll away', there's a similarly picturesque but much calmer spot only half a mile up the coast, at the port of Cellardyke.

Part of the charm of this historic village comes from the fact that it's so hard to find: now effectively merged with the community of Anstruther, Cellardyke lacks the dubious benefit of its own tourist signage. Travellers' confusion is not helped by the fact that it's also known as Lower Kilrenny, and that maps still mark the harbour with its old name of Skinfast Haven. With its rows of traditional houses squeezed into the long, narrow space between sea and cliffside, it could also be called 'the lang toun', if that nickname weren't already taken (see ch. 45).

The original harbour was formed around 1452 with techniques used in Dutch dyke-building. Pilgrims were once ferried from here to St Andrews Cathedral, and the bishop's castle stood close by. Major improvements were made in 1829, including excavations to deepen the harbour basin, and extensive repairs were carried out in both 1898 and 1996 after severe storm damage. Though it's difficult to believe as you survey today's tranquil scene, in the late 19th century Cellardyke was the second most important fishing port in Scotland. The name is said to be a corruption of 'siller [silver] dykes', words that evoke the numerous fishing nets once spread out to dry around the harbour, shining with scales of herring. Nowadays, you might well see more mundane items hanging there: Shore Street residents have long had the right to put their washing out on the lines along the quayside, and many still do, to the delight of visitors who stop by in search of a 'quaint' photo opportunity.

Address Cellardyke, Anstruther, KY10 3AX | **Getting there** Bus 95 to Anstruther (March Crescent); walk south to Tolbooth Wynd, turn left into John Street and keep going for about 5 minutes along the narrow road. You'll pass some fine examples of typical East Neuk houses, some with traditional forestairs. | **Tip** For those seeking more energetic pursuits, East Neuk Outdoors is a family-run outdoor activity centre based at Cellardyke Park, offering sessions for adults and children in everything from kayaking and paddleboarding to archery and bushcraft (www.eastneukoutdoors.co.uk).

62 Fife Folk Museum
A vivid tribute to ordinary lives

Museums that are the fruits of voluntary enterprise have quite a different flavour from those managed by public authorities. The best of them are 'amateur' in the most positive sense: born out of love for a particular subject, and developed by dedicated individuals fired with real enthusiasm and a refreshingly independent approach.

Fife is fortunate indeed to have one shining exemplar: its Folk Museum, established over 50 years ago by a local society intent on preserving artefacts connected with ordinary working people of vanished generations, and bringing them to life through exhibitions and educational initiatives. Over the years, their sterling efforts have attracted funding that has enabled the museum to grow exponentially, and garner several prestigious awards; in 2010, it was granted the accolade of full official accreditation, while continuing to be run almost entirely by volunteers from the local community.

The museum is delightfully situated around the High Street of the lovely old village of Ceres. It incorporates weavers' cottages, a terraced garden, a popular tearoom in the glazed extension overlooking Ceres Burn and, at its core, the atmospheric 17th-century tolbooth, or Weigh House. 'Trading standards' used to be checked here on market days, and it now houses a variety of historic scales and measures. There's a prison cell in the basement, and outside, a chained metal collar, or 'jougs', for the pillorying of offenders. Among the 10,000-odd items in the museum's collection is a comprehensive selection of tools associated with rural trades, plus costume, fine art and all kinds of material related to domestic life of the past three centuries. The thoughtful and effective displays include a reconstructed cottar's living room, and there are intriguing activities for all ages, including 'postcard trails' following the lives of individuals who would otherwise be lost to oblivion. Don't miss the caricature of a local piper by 18th-century stonemason John Howie.

Address High Street, Ceres, KY15 5NF, +44 (0)1334 828180, www.fifefolkmuseum.org | Getting there Bus 64 or X61 to Ceres (Bow Butts) | Hours Apr–Oct, Wed–Sun 10.30am–4pm; tearoom normally open daily all year (but phone to check) | Tip The museum shop has an inexpensive illustrated leaflet on sale to help guide you on a heritage trail around Ceres – described by one authority, with some justification, as the most attractive village in Scotland. Among the many sights worth seeking out is the bizarre 'Toby jug' statue known as the Provost of Ceres, also by John Howie.

63 Wemyss Ware

Cheerful pottery pets with a Bohemian past

The little bulldog seems to blush with embarrassed pleasure as his mistress, holding him gently by the paw, covers his body with vibrant sunflowers. Meanwhile, a gaggle of perky cats eagerly await their turns to be embellished with their signature smiles, while in a nearby room a cluster of chubby pigs emerge from their biscuit firing, impatient to be adorned with cabbage roses. Welcome to the enchanting world of Wemyss Ware pottery.

This unique style of hand-painted ceramics was created in 1882 at the Kirkcaldy pottery of the enterprising Robert Heron, and named in honour of his local aristocratic patrons. It was Heron's idea to invite skilled artists over from Bohemia to develop a new range of practical and decorative wares with brightly coloured, naturalistic motifs of flowers, fruit and cockerels. The gifted designer Karel Nekola soon became head decorator; it was he who introduced the floridly decorated pigs, symbols of good luck in Bohemia, though the bright-eyed, beaming, yellow cats that became one of the most popular Wemyss lines were based on a design by the French artist Emile Gallé. But changes in fashion led to the closure of the Fife works in 1932. Nekola's son and successor Joseph then moved to Devon, taking his secrets to another pottery, which in its turn closed 25 years later.

Wemyss Ware came home to Fife in 1985, when artist Griselda Hill set up her studio in Ceres. Inspired by a Wemyss pig of her grandmother's that she'd loved as a child, she soon got to grips with the unusual underglaze technique, and gained precious insights from her mentor Esther Weeks, protégée of Joseph Nekola. Griselda's studio now owns the Wemyss trademark, and along with her team of four 'Pottery Ladies' she continues to create delightful variants of the classic designs. If you become the proud owner of one of their unique creations you will be in illustrious company: collectors have included Elton John, Gore Vidal and the late Queen Mother.

Address Griselda Hill Pottery, Kirkbrae, Ceres, KY15 5ND, +44 (0)1334 828273, www.wemyss-ware.co.uk | **Getting there** Bus 64 or X61 to Ceres (Bow Butts) | **Hours** Shop & Visitor Centre (with views into the studio): Mon–Sat 2–4.30pm | **Tip** The nearby parish church of Ceres, which dates from 1806, has a lovely interior, with a rare horseshoe-shaped gallery and original oak box pews. An unusually well preserved recumbent stone figure of a medieval knight, from an earlier church on the site, is in the vestibule. Excellent homemade jam is often on sale.

64 The Dutch Village
Fairy tales can come true

It doesn't look remotely Dutch (there's not a windmill in sight), nor does it actually resemble a village – but never mind its prosaic misnomer. The whimsical cluster of towers and turrets on the islet in Craigtoun Country Park has a magical quality that seems straight out of a fairy tale, particularly when glimpsed through the thicket on the bank of its shimmering lake, as a bevy of swans glides around the walls and under the hump-back bridge. Completed a century ago, in an eclectic style best described as Franco-German, the village was the work of architect Paul Waterhouse, part of his remodelling of what was then the Mount Melville estate, for brewing magnate James Younger. The buildings were designed as a fanciful summerhouse and boathouse; the small artificial lake is one of two created to meet insurance company demands for a ready source of water, in case of fire at Younger's vast new mansion. Other features of Waterhouse's scheme that can still be enjoyed today include an Italian Garden and a magnificent avenue of cypresses.

The transformation of the estate into picturesque parkland had in fact begun in the 18th century, when it was the property of the remarkable General Robert Melville, a distinguished soldier who was also an antiquary and a pioneering botanist. Some 230 trees were purchased in 1790 for orchards and other plantings, and landscaping continued under the estate's 19th-century owners, with the creation of woodland belts and attractive vistas.

In 1947, a 47-acre portion of the grounds was sold to Fife Council, who turned it into Scotland's first public country park, under its original name of Craigtoun. Attractions such as a miniature railway and a putting green were added as well as a 'fairy glen', and with rowing boats and pedalos available for hire on the lake, the Dutch Village (which once housed a café) became a favourite spot for generations of locals and holidaymakers.

Address Craigtoun Country Park, KY16 8NX, +44 (0)1334 472013, www.friendsofcraigtoun.org.uk | **Getting there** Bus 64 to Craigtoun Park Lodge, then walk up the drive to the car park and main entrance. The Dutch Village is to the right, in the south-east of the park. | **Hours** Park: unrestricted; village viewable from the outside only | **Tip** The park has a variety of all-year free-use activities for children, as well as seasonal ticketed attractions including the miniature railway, crazy golf, etc. (Apr–Oct; see website for opening times).

65 Crail Airfield

Spy school for literati

If you approach the deserted runways of Crail Airfield just as the haar (sea mist) is rolling in over the fields, it's quite easy to visualise yourself as a bit-part player in a Cold War espionage film, waiting for a downbeat antihero in a raincoat to emerge from the gloom. What makes such an imaginary drama all the more tantalising is that in the 1950s this site was the unlikely home of an élite military academy, the Joint Services School for Linguists (JSSL), where raw conscripts were taught 'a surreal cocktail of arms training and Russian lessons', in the words of one former pupil. This was the time of National Service, when young British men were required to serve for a period in the armed forces; the 5,000 selected for JSSL training were bookish types, deemed capable both of gaining fluency in the Russian language and of eavesdropping on the activities of the Soviets.

Crail Airfield was constructed at the beginning of World War II, for training pilots of the Fleet Air Arm in the art of flying low over water and dropping torpedoes; it remains one of the best-preserved World War II airfields in the UK. After outgrowing two earlier facilities in southern England, the JSSL was established here in 1955, and the following year there were over 700 students living on the outskirts of the East Neuk fishing village. The teaching staff were a group of melancholy emigré Russians who had fled communism, such as the cultivated Prince Volkonsky, who carried a gold-tipped cane, and Colonel Godlevski, who reminisced about drinking champagne from ballerinas' slippers. All were so manifestly depressed that the messroom gained the nickname 'Heartbreak House'.

Some Crail alumni did indeed become career spies, including double agent Geoffrey Prime. Several others, notably Alan Bennett, Dennis Potter and Michael Frayn, went on to considerable fame as writers, making good use of their grounding in Russian literature, and of their insights into the business of deception.

Address Old Airfield, Crail, KY10 3XL | Getting there Bus 95 to Crail, then a 20-minute walk north-east up Balcomie Road | Hours Buildings viewable from the outside only. Some belong to a pig farm; the rest of the site is run by Crail Raceway, who use it for motor sport events and car boot sales (see www.crailraceway.co.uk). | Tip Crail Museum has a room devoted to the airfield, with an archive of historic photos and artefacts. Run by knowledgeable volunteers, the museum also has good displays on many aspects of life in the ancient burgh (62–64 Marketgate, www.crailmuseum.org.uk; summer, Thu–Sat 11am–4pm).

66 __ The Lobster Hut

The freshest crustaceans on the loveliest harbour

There's some stiff competition for the accolade of most picturesque harbour in the East Neuk, but the all-time winner is surely that of Crail. The picture-postcard view of its curved, rampart-like walls, below the neat white and red patchwork of the waterfront cottages, must be the most frequently reproduced image of the Fife coastline (rivalling even the blowy beach of Jack Vettriano's *The Singing Butler*). It has long been a favourite subject for artists' prints, jigsaw puzzles, tea towels and the like – there's even a stately Scottish country dance called Crail Harbour.

Crail is the best preserved of Scotland's ancient seaside Royal Burghs. The town grew up around the port, growing in wealth as a centre for trade as well as fishing, the mainstay of its economy until tourism took over. Salted herring was once an important export, together with Crail capon, a type of dried, smoked haddock, charmingly immortalised in the weathervane crowning the old tolbooth. You won't find either of those fishy specialities on the quayside today, but what you will see is a little wooden hut selling the freshest lobster that anyone could wish for, cooked to order – you can select your own from the open tank – and available to take away or eat right there, at one of the picnic tables overlooking the harbour. Established in 1974, the Lobster Hut is run by the Reilly family, whose local fishing credentials go back for generations. The menu choice is lobster or crab, the pick of the day's catch, fished in creels off Fife Ness by brothers Graeme and Raymond Reilly from their boat *Comely II*. Creel fishing is, incidentally, an environmentally sustainable, species-selective activity with a very low carbon footprint.

If you're looking for frills with your shellfish, there are other, considerably pricier establishments in nearby towns that you might prefer – but be warned that their crustaceans are likely to have been imported from foreign seas.

Address 34 Shoregate, Crail, KY10 3SU, +44 (0)1333 450476, www.facebook.com/reillyshellfish |
Getting there Bus 95 to Crail (Westgate); follow signpost to harbour | Hours Apr–Sept,
Tue–Sun noon–4pm; may vary due to weather conditions | Tip The hut sells soft drinks but no
alcohol; if you want quality wine or beer to accompany your picnic, Green's at 14 High Street sells
a good selection, as well as produce including tasty local fruit and vegetables. Also well worth a
visit is the Smoke Fired Wholefoods Shop opposite, which has a small selection of craft ceramics.

67 Priory Doocot

Impeccable apartments for pigeons

Observant visitors touring the Kingdom may be intrigued by the quantity of curious windowless towers to be seen dotted around the byways, often standing in splendid isolation in the middle of a field. Though always 'traditional' in appearance, they come in a variety of shapes, sizes and styles, from solidly functional to flamboyantly decorative. Some are well preserved, others semi-ruinous and overgrown, but all share the same interior characteristic: their walls are completely lined with a grid of small, deep compartments, designed for occupancy by 'doos' – rock doves or pigeons.

Known as doocots, these pigeon houses were introduced to Scotland in the early 15th century. They became an essential feature of life for hundreds of years thereafter, enshrined in law and protected by superstition, both of which precluded their demolition. The birds were an important food source, providing both eggs and meat, especially in the winter months, but that wasn't all: their feathers and down were used for pillows and mattresses, and the dung was highly valued as an agricultural fertiliser, a softening agent for leather, and even an ingredient of gunpowder. In 1503, it became a legal requirement for Scottish landowners to erect doocots on their properties; they developed into status symbols, and those still standing today are often the only reminder of lost country estates.

Crail's delightful Priory Doocot dates from c1550 and is of the simple 'beehive' type (see also ch. 1). It is exceptional in having been recently and beautifully restored as an educational resource, complete with revolving access ladder, or 'potence', and excellent information panels (plus a surprise when you open the door). Fife has over a quarter of Scotland's surviving doocots, with 106 examples, all of them unique designs. The beehive shape gave way in the 17th century to the sloping-roofed 'lectern' style, and other variants included round and octagonal extravaganzas.

Address Off Nethergate, Crail, KY10 3TY | Getting there Bus 95 to Crail (Marketgate); walk down Kirk Wynd and continue on the path towards the coast | Hours Daily 9am – dusk | Tip The unusual 18th-century Melville Doocot was built as a windmill and later converted; it's also been restored, with a potence ladder in the interior. It's beside the busy A 91, immediately west of the junction with the A 92 (Melville Gates roundabout); access is by key, obtainable from Windmill Cottage opposite.

68 Dunino Den

Reconnecting with the elementals

Fife is exceptionally rich in atmospheric places that are strongly redolent of the distant past. Some of these are well documented and
securely dateable, but there are other ancient sites where the very
absence of material evidence only seems to add to the tantalising
genius loci, or spirit of the place. Dunino Den is one such spot: a sacred
grove by a stream, enclosed in a craggy gorge, that has all the hall-
marks of a Celtic place of worship, though the man-made features
of the site are impossible to date.

The den is reached from a short path behind Dunino Kirk – an
attractive neo-Gothic building on the site of a considerably older
church – that leads to the rocky promontory of Bel Craig. (As with
the nearby settlement of Beley, where a stone circle once stood, this
name probably indicates an association with the Celtic sun god, Bel.)
Carved into a flat expanse of rock is a deep-looking well and a shallow footprint, uncovered when the site was investigated in 1845. From
here a flight of steps cut into the bedrock descends into a peaceful
wooded dell by a trickling burn, sheltered by towering red sandstone
cliffs, moulded over aeons into shapes that must have held meaning
for ancient peoples. Later generations have added carvings of a ringed
Celtic cross, a green man and other symbols.

All around are signs of the awe and respect that the site still
evokes for modern-day pagan pilgrims – small personal mementoes
discreetly placed on clefts in trees, branches festooned with ribbons
and 'clooties' (colourful strips of cloth), rows of coins set into the
naturally weathered orifices on the crags.

As the breeze stirs the high leafy canopy and the sunlight glances
off the rippling water, even the most resolutely non-spiritual visitor
will surely be entranced by the timeless magic of the place, and the
salutary sensation that it brings of reconnection with an enduring
natural continuum.

Address Dunino, KY16 8LU | Getting there Bus X60 to Dunino Primary School and a 10-minute walk south-east – follow signs to Dunino Kirk. A short path from the church car park leads past the graveyard to the den. (NB The ancient rock-cut steps are narrow, steep and slippery if wet.) | Tip By the southern wall of the graveyard is a 'wishing stone' – a flat-topped, sculpted block, thought to date from the 9th century, covered in oxidising coins. Leave your own monetary offering while you envisage your hopes and desires.

69 The Chain Walk

Step we gaily, on we go

Its name might suggest a Scottish country dance, but don't let that mislead you: although it does require some fancy footwork, there is absolutely no skipping, reeling or setting to your partner involved in doing the Chain Walk. Furthermore, fuelling yourself with a wee dram beforehand is definitely not on the cards, for the 'walk' in question is in fact a rock climb, involving scrambling, clambering, hiking and crawling your way for nearly a third of a mile along a route that snakes round the steep coastal cliffs at Kincraig Point, west of Elie, assisted by eight lengths of solidly planted steel chains, both horizontal and vertical, and some well-placed footholds. That said, it's an attraction that can be enjoyed by any fit, agile, intrepid individual with a good head for heights.

The route was created in 1929, commissioned from a local blacksmith by a group of Elie and Earlsferry residents, who raised £100 for the project. It's said that it was originally intended for the use of fishermen, but it clearly also had a recreational function. Though often described as Fife's own *via ferrata* – a term used for alpine routes enhanced by cables, rungs and other climbing aids – it does not require any mountaineering equipment; stout footwear, suitable clothing, proper preparation and common sense are however all essential. The most important thing to bear in mind is that the route should only be undertaken when the sea is out, or at least receding, since it becomes immersed at high tide.

Up to two hours should be allowed to appreciate all that it has to offer. Your reward is an exhilarating adventure that takes in three caves (including one where Macduff allegedly hid while fleeing from Macbeth) spectacular basalt columns, rock pools, sea birds and panoramic views across the Firth of Forth.

Return via the cliff-top path and you'll also see the extensive remains of wartime defences, including gun emplacements.

Address West Bay, Elie, KY9; Elie Newsagents, 50 High Street, has a leaflet on the Chain Walk route | **Getting there** Bus 95 or X60 to Elie High Street; walk west on Bank Street, Earlsferry High Street and across the golf course, then follow the beach towards the headland | **Hours** Check tide times online beforehand; start no later than two hours before high tide | **Tip** The starter's hut on Elie golf links is equipped with a 30-foot-high periscope, salvaged in the 1960s from the submarine HMS *Excalibur*, an experimental vessel powered by hydrogen peroxide. It allows club officials to ensure that players can tee off at the first hole without hitting other golfers (www.golfhouseclub.co.uk).

70 Lady's Tower

The flighty bather who flattened a village

Janet Fall was quite a lady. A fashionable beauty with a reputation as a flirt, she was painted more than once by society favourite Sir Joshua Reynolds; his 1761 portrait (now in the Tate Gallery) shows her as she would like to be remembered – luxuriantly dressed in pink satin, posing proprietarily in the grounds of her husband's Fife estate. In the lore of the East Neuk, however, her chief memorial is the legacy of her arrogant, high-handed behaviour: the lost hamlet of Balclevie, demolished on her instructions to improve the view from her house (an act for which her descendants were cursed), and the tower she had built to indulge her private passion.

Born in 1727, Janet was the daughter of James Fall of Dunbar, one of four brothers who established a powerful and prosperous mercantile dynasty. This brought them a social elevation that was remarkable, for they were said to have close blood ties to Scotland's gypsy kings, the Faa family. In 1750, Janet married Sir John Anstruther, laird of Ardross and Elie, but rumours of her lowly origins dogged her aristocratic life. Nicknamed 'Jenny Faa' by the populace, she was mocked at the hustings for her husband's parliamentary election by a crowd singing 'The Gypsy Laddie'.

In 1771 the Anstruthers decided to make improvements to their estate, which included building a summerhouse on a headland above a little cove, with a rocky, vaulted chamber below. Sea bathing – in the nude – had lately become a craze among the upper classes, for its alleged health-giving benefits, and Janet demanded an appropriate undressing room. Her outings were signalled by a servant ringing a handbell, warning locals to steer clear – a procedure then current for segregated bathing sessions at public resorts. Now Janet's tower is roofless, intriguingly weathered and open to all. It's a fabulous spot to discover on a bright, bracing day, with the Bass Rock on the horizon, shimmering with the plumage of its vast gannet colony.

Address Ruby Bay, Elie, KY9 1BJ | Getting there Bus 95 or X60 to Elie High Street; walk down Wadeslea to Ruby Bay, then follow Fife Coastal Path | Hours Unrestricted | Tip The sandy cove of Ruby Bay is so called because of the tiny blood-red gemstones that can still be found on the beach – not actual rubies, but a type of garnet known as pyrope, washed ashore from the ancient volcanic rocks in which they're embedded. On a sunny day you may spot some glinting between the low and high tide lines, if you get very close to the gravelly sand.

71__The Cheese Farm
The fresh tang of the East Neuk

Scottish cheese has its own history, quite distinct from that of England. Though dairy produce was always part of the Scots diet, the varieties consumed here were mostly restricted to soft, cottage-type crowdie and rich, creamy caboc, until the cheddar-style Dunlop appeared in the 17th century. But, as in the rest of the UK, all Scottish farmhouse cheeses suffered a drastic decline in the 20th century, disappearing entirely for a time until the great revival of traditional cheesemaking began in the 1980s.

Jane Stewart of Falside brought Fife into the revolution in 2008, when she created the fresh, tangy, crumbly Anster (so called from the local pronunciation of the nearby town of Anstruther, which is actually closer to AINster). Both she and her husband Robert come from experienced East Neuk dairy-farming families, but since no farmhouse cheesemaking was going on locally, Jane went to Wales to learn the subtleties of the age-old craft. Still a popular favourite, Anster has since been joined by three sister varieties – red (with garlic and chives), mature and smoked – plus a sharp and nutty cousin, the multi-award-winning St Andrews Cheddar. These are all available from the farm shop, along with a small selection of complementary produce.

For many years, the building where the cheeses begin life also housed a lovely coffee shop, with a glazed viewing area where visitors could observe the slow transformation of the raw milk. Sadly, the café is no longer open on a regular basis, but pre-booked parties are welcome to visit for an illuminating talk about the making process, followed by a cheese platter and the farm's legendary homemade cheese scones. The outdoor terrace has a fabulous open vista down to the coast and beyond, and if you're lucky the foreground might include a group of the piebald Holstein Friesians who are at the heart of the business, grazing contentedly or eyeing you inquisitively.

Address St Andrews Farmhouse Cheese Company, Falside, near Anstruther, KY10 2RT, +44 (0)1333 312580, www.standrewscheese.co.uk | Getting there Off B 9171, 2.5 miles north of Pittenweem (NB Despite the farm's trading name, it is *not* in the town of St Andrews) | Hours Shop: Mon–Fri 10am–2pm (takeaway coffee and tea available); for café bookings email info@standrewscheese.co.uk | Tip About a mile east of Falside, off a minor road near the junction with the B9131, look out for a tall octagonal tower standing in the middle of a field. This is the extraordinarily ornate West Pitkierie doocot, built in the 18th century to house pigeons for the owners of a long-gone mansion (see ch 67).

72 The Cambo Snowdrops
Carpets of milk flowers

Galanthophilia is a pervasive condition that has seen a marked rise in recent years. It reaches its peak in the gloomy days of February, but it has nothing to do with the winter blues – quite the reverse, in fact. Those who succumb to this contagion are a particular breed of plant enthusiast who develop an all-consuming passion for the dainty little flower whose blooming signals the promise of spring: *Galanthus*, known to lesser mortals as the snowdrop.

The 'milk flower' (as the botanical name translates) is not native to these shores. The naturalised *G. nivalis* seems to have been introduced in the 16th century, but it was in the 1850s that the British obsession took off, when soldiers returning from the Crimean War brought back bulbs of *G. plicatus*.

Today, around 20 species are known, but within these there are up to 3,000 cultivars, and collectors are willing to pay hundreds of pounds for particularly sought-after specimens. Many varieties differ only by what non-*aficionados* might consider trivial differences in size or in the green flecking at the end of the petals, but the more unusual can have pretty green markings on the outside, and some have yellow stalks or even yellow-streaked heads.

Fife is blessed with a paradise for galanthophiles at Cambo, an extensive country estate near Kingsbarns that is home to the UK's National Collection of snowdrops, with over 350 varieties. Lady Catherine Erskine set up her mail order business here in 1986, with the USP of selling snowdrops while in leaf rather than as dried bulbs in the autumn; her team now sends out hundreds of thousands of plants 'in the green' every year to gardeners all over the UK.

But you don't have to be a fanatic to simply enjoy a stroll through the woodland along Cambo Burn, where you can revel in the innumerable dazzling hosts of tiny white periscopes that carpet its banks from late January to early March.

Address Cambo Gardens, Kingsbarns, KY16 8QD, +44 (0)1333 451040, www.cambogardens.org.uk | Getting there Off A 917, south-east of Kingsbarns; bus 95 to Cambo Lodge and a 20-minute walk | Hours Daily 10am–5pm; Snowdrop Festival (with sales, tours and workshops) late Jan–early Mar | Tip The grand Cambo House was rebuilt in the 1880s after the original historic pile burnt down, following a riotous staff party while the family were away. It now offers a wide range of visitor accommodation for holidays, weddings, etc. (www.camboestate.com).

73 Alexander Selkirk

Dances with cats

The fantasy of being marooned on a desert island is a trope that runs deep in our collective imagination, epitomised for evermore in the redoubtable figure of Robinson Crusoe, whose castaway 'memoir' originally appeared in 1719. A phenomenal and vastly influential bestseller, it was only later revealed to be a work of fiction by the journalist and political propagandist Daniel Defoe.

It was the adventures of a Fifer named Alexander Selkirk that provided the springboard for Defoe's novel. An independent-minded seaman, Selkirk had been put ashore voluntarily in 1704 on the rugged little island of Más a Tierra, off the coast of Chile, following a row with his tyrannical captain about the seaworthiness of their privateer galley. It would be well over four years before he was rescued. Selkirk was resourceful, but he had no Man Friday, and the fact that he survived his solitary exile so well was thanks in large measure to two species of mammal introduced by earlier explorers. A tribe of feral cats slept with him in his pimento-wood hut, protecting him from ravening rats, while goats supplied him with milk, meat and skins for clothing. Singing and dancing in the company of his four-legged friends was his chief diversion from despair. The castaway became a celebrity on his return to the newly unified Britain of 1709; he spent some years in London and Bristol (where he may have met Defoe) before returning for a time to his home town of Lower Largo.

Records reveal Selkirk as a wayward rogue with many failings, estranged from his family and an unabashed bigamist. Nonetheless, the statue erected in 1885 on the site of his birthplace shows a heroic figure, a sturdy colonialist in Crusoe mode, surveying the scene from his vantage point above the doorway like a guerrilla fighter on sentry duty – far from the wiry, wild-eyed, manic creature described by his rescuers. Regrettably, sculptor T.S. Burnett did not see fit to include a vigilant cat or a frisky kid in his composition.

Address 101/103 Main Street, Lower Largo, KY8 6BJ | Getting there Bus 95, 97, 395 or X60 to Lower Largo (Durham Wynd); the sculpture is signposted, annoyingly, as 'Robinson Crusoe Statue' | Tip The adjacent village of Upper Largo was the home of the illustrious sailor Sir Andrew Wood, 'Scotland's Nelson', who commanded the Scottish naval fleet against the English in 1513. There is still evidence of the quarter-mile-long canal that he had built to connect his castle to the local church, so that he could sail there, with due ceremony, by barge.

74 Lundin Ladies' Golf Club

Elusive links with prehistory

Fife is a golfer's nirvana, with over 50 courses in locations ranging from rugged clifftops to rolling parks that cater to all levels of ability. There's even one that might intrigue many of the game's most avowed detractors – though for reasons that have little to do with the business of whacking a wee ball with a big stick into a series of holes around a field.

The Ladies' Golf Club in Lundin Links is one of the oldest in the world with an exclusively female membership. Constituted in 1891, the club moved in 1910 to its present nine-hole course, designed by the renowned James Braid, after its members were asked to vacate their previous location in order to give Lundin's gentlemen golfers the room to manspread. The ladies' new site was aptly called Standing Stanes Park, for right in the middle of what is now the manicured sward of the second fairway are three colossal prehistoric megaliths, the remains of a ceremonial centre of tremendous significance to the people who lived in this area around 4,000 years ago. Records show that there was originally a fourth stone, giving grounds for the theory that the group was a 'four-poster' – a stone circle that was more of a stone rectangle. It's likely that it once had an astronomical purpose, focused on Largo Law, though its complex meaning changed for subsequent generations. A legend of dubious date connects the place with medieval scholar Michael Scot, a wandering polymath who became mythologised as a powerful wizard.

You have to spend time contemplating the formidable trio (golfers permitting) to begin to appreciate – as our ancestors would have done – their anthropomorphic presence and subtle interrelationship. Watching their shape-shifting shadows, you might fancy you hear the breeze whispering, 'When shall we three meet again?', as the weird sisters of Shakespeare's 'Scottish play' drift through your mind.

Address Woodielea Road, Lundin Links, KY8 6AR, +44 (0)1333 320832, www.lundinladiesgolfclub.co.uk | **Getting there** Bus 95, 97 or X60 to Leven Road (Lundin Links Hotel); the Ladies' Club is signposted (NB do not confuse with Lundin Golf Club). Ask at the hut by the entrance before walking to the stones. Golfers of all genders are welcome to play the course, on payment of green fees | **Hours** Always open, but avoid Wed up till 2pm, when club competitions are held | **Tip** The gift shop and café Jane's at Nineteen is a congenial spot for refreshment, with the likely bonus of a chat with a few ladies of Lundin (19 Leven Road, KY8 6AQ).

75 Bowbridge Alpacas
Close encounters of the camelid kind

They could hardly be further from the Peruvian *altiplano*, but the alpacas grazing peacefully in the rolling countryside of north-east Fife seem quite at home here. The South American camelids, domesticated from the wild vicuña around 7,000 years ago, first appeared on British farms in the 1990s (although their much-prized wool had a significant prior history in the UK, as the source of the wealth of Victorian cloth magnate Titus Salt). Though often mistaken for their cousin the llama, alpacas are only half their size, and this, together with their docile nature and exceptionally soft coats, is undoubtedly part of their appeal. When they turn their graceful necks to meet your gaze with their gorgeous, long-lashed almond eyes, you just won't be able to stop smiling.

For a hands-on encounter, with the privilege of bonding with one of these intelligent, biddable creatures, book a visit to Bowbridge Farm, where Sarah Johnson will guide you through an immersive experience with the herd. This includes hand feeding (quite safe, as they have no top front teeth) and an introduction to training techniques, and culminates in leading your chosen alpaca on a trek round the farm, part of it through an obstacle course. You'll learn a lot about their behaviour, such as their fastidious habit of using a communal 'field toilet', and as a final treat have a go at needle-felting a little of their luxuriant wool. High quality knitting yarn is also on sale.

The Johnson family began their venture in 2015, after former dancer Sarah had gained experience working on alpaca farms in Europe. Her father Paul had already undertaken a handling course where he became aware of the stress-relieving value of alpaca encounters, and these have always been part of the farm's remit. A group of Bowbridge's finest are regularly booked for therapeutic visits to local care homes, schools and the like, and they've even starred as camels in nativity plays, to the delight of audience and participants.

Address Bowbridge Farm, Peat Inn, KY15 5LL, +44 (0)7484 778040, www.bowbridgealpacas.com | **Getting there** On B 941, 0.6 mile south-east of Peat Inn | **Hours** 1- & 2-hour Alpaca Experiences Wed & Fri 2.30pm, Sat 10.30am, 2.30pm; booking essential | **Tip** The hamlet of Peat Inn is famed for its eponymous restaurant with rooms, a multi-award-winning establishment which, in the 1980s, earned the first ever Scottish Michelin star. The 2020 Good Food Guide judged it the second best in Scotland (Peat Inn, KY15 5LH, +44 (0)1334 840206, www.thepeatinn.co.uk).

76__The Arts Festival

Creative endeavour round every corner

There are many reasons why artists are drawn to the East Neuk: the exceptional quality of the light, the infinite moods of the sea and sky, the gentler pace of life and the inspiration to be found all around, in sources from the traditional buildings to the maritime flora, fauna and geology. The community of Pittenweem is a particular focal point: not only does it have over 30 resident visual artists, it's also been home for almost four decades to a flourishing arts festival, now so cherished that it's an integral part of the town's identity. In 2019, it attracted more than 20,000 visitors over eight days, to view the multifarious work of 134 artists.

A major factor in the festival's enduring success is that it has never lost sight of the local roots that make it so special; it's an inclusive event that brings together a great range of styles and media, and although a few guest exhibitors are always invited, none of the art on display is 'juried' by the organisers. Most of it is shown in spaces not normally open to the public, and half the joy comes from seeking out the venues themselves – 99 at the last count – concealed up narrow wynds, behind the venerable façades of the upper town and all along the waterfront. As you head west, the sea captains' houses of East Shore give way, via what is still a busy, working harbour, to fishermen's cottages, humbler but vividly picturesque. A huge variety of premises is pressed into service to display artworks – private homes and studios, ancient garden plots and courtyards, modern garages and sheds, as well as formal galleries and evocatively named venues like the Old Men's Club, the Fish Loft and the Harbourmaster's Office. In 2019, there was even an exhibition offshore, in the lighthouse on the Isle of May (see ch. 59). On the opening day the whole town buzzes with creative energy, as people of all ages and abilities concentrate on producing their entries for the Open Art painting competition, a truly inspirational local event.

Address Festival Office: 47 High Street, Pittenweem, KY10 2PG, +44 (0)1333 313109, www.pittenweemartsfestival.co.uk | **Getting there** Bus 95, X60 to Pittenweem (Tollcross); Festival shuttle bus from Charles Street car park to High Street, harbour and outlying venues | **Hours** Runs for 8 days in Aug, beginning first Sat; most venues 10am–5pm, plus daytime talks and evening events | **Tip** The Festival includes a lively programme of workshops, events and tours, comprising historical and geological walks, artists' talks and evening concerts. Advance booking is advisable.

77 St Fillan's Cave

The shady tale of the man with the luminous arm

Rearing its substantial head over a steep lane in the heart of Pitten-weem is a magnificent outcrop of striated golden sandstone. Such an unruly feature would be anathema to developers today, but this ancient town is the 'place of the cave' going by its etymology – which indicates that these rocks were once central to its very existence. A modern doorway leads into the eponymous *uiamh*, or weem, a nat-ural, Y-shaped formation with a spring in one of its arms, now a mere trickle, but once widely revered as a holy healing well.

Pittenweem was first recorded as a port in 1228, and it's the only East Neuk town that still harbours a thriving fishing fleet. Its origins, however, were on the land above the shore, settled at least 10 centuries ago; the cave became a sacred Christian site and place of pilgrimage, dedicated to Mary Magdalene. The association with St Fillan came much later, probably at the behest of Bishop James Kennedy, the 15th-century commendator of the priory that once occupied an extensive area of land above the cave. He was a devotee of the saint, a popular cult figure since the Scots' victory at Bannockburn in 1314, which many attributed to his miraculous intervention.

Fillan's story is confused by the fact that there were at least two saints by that name, only one of whom was a historic individual, a missionary who came over from Ireland in the 8th century and settled in Perthshire; there is no evidence that he ever came to Fife. None-theless, the legend arose that he had once lived as a hermit in the Pittenweem cave, studying and writing sermons with the aid of his phenomenal left arm, which apparently glowed in the dark.

After the Reformation, the site fell from grace; it was used to stash smugglers' booty and later became a rubbish dump. In 1935, however, it was cleared out and rededicated as a place of worship. The hand-some wrought-iron gate was added in 2000. There is a simple stone altar, and services are still occasionally held there.

Address 12 Cove Wynd, Pittenweem, KY10 2LE | **Getting there** Bus 95 or X60 to Pittenweem (Tollcross) | **Hours** Key obtainable from Cocoa Tree Café, 9 High Street, KY10 2LA, open daily 10am–6pm | **Tip** The nearby tolbooth, which formerly housed council chambers and a jail, was central to an infamous episode in Pittenweem's history. In 1704, the accusations of a 16-year-old boy resulted in 9 arrests for witchcraft, leading to the gruesome, protracted torture of several individuals, and the hideous death of Janet Corphat, killed by a mob of townsfolk after her release from prison.

78 Bell Pettigrew Museum
Sad solitaires, flexible fish and flying machines

Most museums today put only a tiny fraction of their collections on show, usually in pared-down, designer-led displays that direct the attention to a few choice spotlit exhibits. St Andrews University's museum of natural history is beguilingly different: a throwback to a former age of museology, its single gallery is chock-full of a vast array of diverse treasures from the animal kingdom. There are poignant relics of extinct species, from the St Kilda house mouse to the Rodrigues solitaire, a flightless bird related to the dodo that shed tears when captured, and exquisite lobe-finned fossil fish from nearby Dura Den, once believed to be an evolutionary missing link to land creatures. More fishy intrigue can be found in the case devoted to the polymath Professor D'Arcy Thompson, whose 'biological transformations' demonstrated that any species of fish could be theoretically stretched and squeezed until it looked just like some other.

Opened in 1912, the Bell Pettigrew owes its collections to the curiosities accumulated from 1838 onwards by the town's Literary and Philosophical Society, plus many donations from specialists in later decades. But the museum would not exist in its current form had it not been for the generosity of a philanthropic woman, Elsie Bell Pettigrew. An independently wealthy heiress, she selflessly donated the funds for a purpose-built museum in memory of her husband James, the late Professor of Medicine and an important pioneer in the study of flight, who in 1903, at the age of 70, had flown for 20 yards in his flapping 'ornithopter'. A small display in the museum is devoted to specimens of winged creatures, collected and prepared by him for his research. Elsie lavished particular care on the project, insisting on state-of-the-art display cases as used by Harrods, and personally designing the mosaic-tiled floor. But although her monogram appears discreetly on the building's exterior, she was excluded from the grand opening and its men-only banquet.

Address School of Biology, Bute Buildings, St Andrews, KY16 9TS, www.st-andrews.ac.uk | Getting there Bus to St Andrews | Hours Open to visitors during school holidays; email museum-enquiries@st-andrews.ac.uk for details | Tip The delightful museum of social history run by the long-established St Andrews Preservation Trust is a few minutes' walk away at 12 North Street. Housed in a 17th-century cottage, with a secluded garden dedicated to D'Arcy Thompson, it also has extensive photographic archives (opening hours vary – phone +44 (0)1334 477629 or email museum@stapt.org.uk to check.).

79 _ The Botanic Garden

Bright wings in a green oasis

Visitors to St Andrews generally park their cars, or alight from their buses, just to the west of the old burgh limits, and then head straight into the historic town, or down to the illustrious golf links. But if you ignore the pull of the crowds and turn the opposite way instead, you will soon discover a peaceful haven of horticultural delights, whose unfamiliarity to the majority of tourists – as well as a surprising number of locals – is entirely undeserved.

The botanic garden is a fairly recent addition to St Andrews' attractions, at least in its current location. It was originally established by the university in 1889, on plots within St Mary's College which it gradually outgrew. In the 1960s the decision was made to transfer the entire plant collection to an 18-acre site on the banks of the Kinness Burn, then agricultural land.

Now home to over 8,000 species, native and exotic (plus a seaweed herbarium), the garden is a registered collection of national importance, run since 2014 by a charitable trust. It continues to be a focus for botanical conservation and research, as well as a public resource for education, relaxation and enjoyment, among its mature woodlands, meadows, herbaceous borders and glasshouses. The extensive rockery is a particular delight, dotted with jewels of colour, leading down to ponds, trickling falls and a soothing water garden. There's also a thriving urban farm, and a base for community projects promoting the cultivation of produce.

Yet more spiritual replenishment is to be found within the tropical butterfly house, an awe-inspiring space where visitors of all ages are entranced, relaxed and touched (in every sense) by the constant, dazzling display of brilliantly patterned, fluttering wings. It's staffed by welcoming, thoughtful volunteers who care for their delicate charges with a genuine passion, and discuss their extraordinary life cycles with enthusiasm and warmth.

Address Canongate, St Andrews, KY16 8RT, +44 (0)1334 476452, www.standrewsbotanic.org |
Getting there Bus to St Andrews Bus Station; follow Viaduct Walk footpath from Argyle Street
Car Park and turn right on Canongate | Hours Apr–Sept, daily 10am–6pm, Oct–Dec & Mar,
daily 10am–4pm, Jan & Feb, Sat & Sun 10am–4pm (NB Butterfly House closed Oct–Mar) |
Tip St Andrews Museum is well worth a visit for its small but highly absorbing displays on local
history, temporary exhibitions and café. It's in Kinburn Park, a 5-minute walk west of the bus
station (+44 (0)1334 659380, www.onfife.com).

80 The Byre Theatre

Please keep your feet off the stage

The story of what is arguably both the finest and the most attractive small-scale theatre in Scotland is itself the stuff of melodrama.

The Byre had its genesis in 1933, when a group of amateur dramatics enthusiasts from Hope Park Church, led by journalist Alex B. Paterson, were looking for a home for the newly formed St Andrews Play Club. They chanced upon a semi-derelict cowshed, or byre, that had been part of a dairy farm in the burgh, and set about creating the tiny theatre that would house them until 1969, supporting not just their own productions but also a professional repertory season, which fostered the talent of actors such as Edward Woodward. Early audiences made do with cushions on the floor (later replaced with 74 cinema seats) and a hay loft served both as dressing room and scenery store. The stage itself was only 12 feet square; a notice requested playgoers to keep their feet off it. But the extreme proximity of audience to actors was very much part of the experience, and it was not unknown for those in the front row to engage characters in unscripted dialogue during particularly compelling scenes.

In 1970, the lights went up on the Byre's second act when it moved into its next home, an austere new structure close to the original site but with double the capacity. In time, redevelopment was needed to meet modern requirements; the theatre was completely rebuilt from the bottom up, and in 2001 the splendid Byre of today was opened – fittingly, by former milkman Sir Sean Connery – boasting vastly improved facilities while retaining its cherished intimate quality. An unscheduled interlude came in 2013, when financial troubles forced a sudden closure, but in autumn 2014 it reopened under the management of St Andrews University. The much-loved venue now continues in an inclusive town-gown partnership, maintaining its roots in the local community as a focus for all kinds of creativity, professional, student and amateur.

Address Abbey Street, St Andrews, KY16 9LA, +44 (0)1334 475000, www.byretheatre.com | **Getting there** Bus to St Andrews Bus Station and a 10-minute walk, or 64, 92A/B/C/D, 95 or 99A/B to Byre Theatre | **Hours** Daily from 10am | **Tip** Tailend at 130 Market Street is an award-winning restaurant and takeaway owned by G & A Spinks, long-established fish merchants of Arbroath. It offers a range of quality seafood dishes (including their legendary smokies) in addition to traditional Scottish fish suppers, and also has a fresh fish counter (www.thetailend.co.uk)

81 The Cathedral Museum

A hidden Pictish masterpiece with far-flung roots

Languishing in a lesser-known museum within the grounds of St Andrews Cathedral is a masterpiece of sculpture from the Dark Ages that ranks as one of the rarest artistic treasures in Europe. Visitors pass in a regular trickle through the portals of the old ecclesiastical building that houses it, but few pause for long to admire the remarkable work in carved sandstone, the creation of a Pictish artist of over 1,250 years ago. Part of the problem is the way it's displayed, too low down and dimly lit to be properly appreciated, with information panels placed so that the text is barely legible.

Rediscovered in 1833, the ensemble of slabs became known as the St Andrews Sarcophagus, though it's now thought not to be a coffin, but part of a memorial shrine to a Pictish king of the late 8th century, probably Óengus, son of Fergus. It would originally have stood within the earliest monastery on this site, of which no trace remains. The largest panel depicts a busy, symbol-laden scene filled with animals, showing the biblical King David killing a lion, an action echoed by a Pictish king on horseback.

Both the high relief and the content may surprise those who know the Picts only from the eloquent linear art of their free-standing stones; it demonstrates the sculptor's familiarity with both the Celtic tradition of interlaced patterns and the more exotic imagery of the Byzantine empire, which he would probably have known from their exquisite ivory carvings. It's worth noting that the St Andrews panels are very likely to have been brightly painted originally, as was most medieval sculpture.

There is more to explore in this atmospheric little museum: the undercroft has a collection of beautifully carved 17th-century gravestones, plus a rare sketch incised in stone by a medieval mason. Don't miss the haunting tomb slab of Christian Brydie, showing a happy couple in a poignant embrace.

Address St Andrews Cathedral, The Pends, St Andrews, KY16 9QL, +44 (0)1334 472563, www.historicenvironment.scot | Getting there Bus to St Andrews | Hours Daily Apr–Sept 9.30am–5.30pm, Oct–Mar 10am–4pm | Tip Your museum ticket includes entry to the ruins of St Andrews Castle, clifftop residence of Scotland's most powerful churchmen until the Reformation (a 5-minute walk away on The Scores). Intrepid visitors can peer down its grim bottle dungeon and explore its underground tunnels, dug during a siege in 1546–47.

82_ The PH Monogram
Burning with intent

These days, a title like *Patrick's Places* might suggest an easy-viewing TV travel show with some jaunty, facile presenter. But in 1526 it signified a radical publication – a religious tract so dangerous that it sealed the fate of its author, the idealistic young theologian Patrick Hamilton. For the 'places' he listed were commonplaces – self-evident truths – that affirmed the authority of the scriptures in Christian worship and explicitly challenged the power and manifestly corrupt practices of the Catholic clergy.

Patrick came from a noble Scots family; a posthumous portrait shows a sensitive, pensive redhead with a luxuriant beard that would be the envy of modern-day hipsters. It was while studying theology in Paris that he was introduced to the writings of Martin Luther. On his return to Scotland he joined the faculty of arts at St Andrews University, and began preaching the reformed doctrine, soon incurring the wrath of Archbishop James Beaton. After a hasty trial, he was condemned as a heretic and sentenced to be burned at the stake that same day, 29 February, 1528. It may be that Beaton thought, unwisely, that the mere threat of such a hideous death would be enough to make the 24-year-old publicly renounce his beliefs. In any event, his tormentors were ill-prepared: the firewood was damp and inadequate, the weather was blustery, the gunpowder that was laid merely seared his head and hands, and it was a full six hours before the stoic and unrepentant Patrick's ghastly ordeal was over.

Rather than defending free speech, the university upheld the position of the church and helped to convict Hamilton. That is presumably why undergraduates still shun the monogram in stone setts that marks the site of his martyrdom. According to student lore, those who step on the letters are sure to fail their final exams; the only way to lift the curse is to undergo a chilly ordeal by water, in the annual dawn May Day dip in the North Sea.

Address St Salvator's Chapel, North Street, St Andrews, KY16 9AL | **Getting there** Bus to St Andrews; the monogram is on the pavement opposite the archway under St Salvator's tower | **Tip** High above the coat of arms on the tower is a ghostly face, said to be the image of Patrick Hamilton, ominously etched into the stonework at the time of his death. A few minutes' walk away, on the roadside outside St Andrews Castle, another stone monogram, almost submerged in asphalt, marks the site of the burning of the town's next Protestant martyr, George Wishart, in 1546.

83 ___ The R&A World Golf Museum

Open secrets right by the Old Course

It's the holy grail of golf – or an authorised replica of it, at any rate. The Claret Jug is, rightfully, the culminating exhibit of the R & A World Golf Museum, a low-key, bunker-like building in St Andrews, situated within striking distance of the Royal & Ancient clubhouse and the first tee of the Old Course. There couldn't be a more appropriate site for a museum devoted to the history of the game: it's been played here since at least the 15th century, and as early as 1691 the town was referred to as the 'metropolis of golfing'. The coveted silver trophy, presented annually to the winner of the Open Championship, is no doubt the museum's star exhibit for true *aficionados*, but even the uninitiated, or those with only a casual interest in the sport, will find a surprising variety of other highlights among the eclectic displays. With a total of over 17,000 items, this is Europe's largest collection of golfing memorabilia.

The story of the world's most popular ball and stick game, from its medieval beginnings up to the present day, is told in a circuit of themed galleries. Topics include pioneering women players and golfing fashion, as well as an exhaustive typology of equipment, from the oldest set of clubs in the world to the latest in high-tech gee-whizzery. Intriguing items catch the eye at every turn, such as the Silver Club, a trophy covered in a mass of glittering balls like an over-the-top Christmas ornament, and the two-tone trousers worn by Gary Player at the 1960 Open, as a protest against apartheid. There's a striking recreation of the workshop of a famous Victorian ball maker, from the days when a top hat-full of feathers was laboriously stuffed into each little leather casing, and a practice room where you can try out various types of ball and old-style putters, plus a host of activities for younger visitors that are both fun and informative.

Address Bruce Embankment, St Andrews, KY16 9AB, +44 (0)1334 460046, www.worldgolfmuseum.com | **Getting there** Bus to St Andrews Bus Station | **Hours** Daily 10am–4pm; The Niblick restaurant 9.30am–5pm (Sun from 10am); free admission for children | **Tip** On the shore 2 minutes' walk away is St Andrews Aquarium, home to a wide variety of wonderful aquatic creatures including penguins, crocodiles, octopuses, seals, sharks and piranhas as well as, rather unexpectedly, meerkats and marmosets (daily 10am–5pm).

The Golf Champion Trophy, better known as the Claret Jug, was first presented to Tom Kidd at St Andrews in 1873, the first time The Open had been played outside Prestwick. With no prize to present to him the year

84 The Rock and Spindle

The explosive past of a peaceful shore

What does it remind *you* of? Extraordinary natural phenomena defy neat description, yet something deep in our collective psyche compels us to look for associations that bring them into a more recognisable, human-friendly world. So it is with this powerful geological wonder at Kinkell Ness near St Andrews: some might see the tall stack as a petrified tree trunk or, inevitably, a phallic symbol, while the radial disc inspires comparisons with everything from a giant daisy to a fractured rose window from some primeval cathedral.

Generations ago, the twin components came to be known as the Rock and Spindle because of their perceived resemblance to a pair of everyday objects used in hand spinning to make yarn. 'Rock', it must be explained, is another word for 'distaff', a long wooden tool that would be wrapped with a mass of combed wool or flax; the fibres were then slowly twisted and wound on to a short stick weighted with a disc-shaped whorl – the spindle. Spinning of this kind was an exclusively female task, carried out by women of all classes, and for countless centuries these tools were a very familiar sight, not just in Fife but around the world.

Imagining that some giant earth mother has just put down her work for the day is a great deal less alarming than contemplating the violent reality of how this stunning feature was actually formed. Around 350 million years ago Fife was quite literally a hotbed of geological activity, with small volcanoes erupting on land and at sea, forcing molten magma through soft deposits of sandstone. The Rock and Spindle is what geologists call a volcanic neck, formed from magma that solidified inside the pipes of the Kinkell Ness volcano's plumbing system, and was exposed over millennia as the surrounding rock was eroded away.

The geological facts may take away from the mystery of the place, but they don't make it any less awesome.

Address Kinkell Ness, St Andrews, KY16 | **Getting there** Bus to St Andrews, then walk through the town beyond the cathedral to the harbour. Cross the footbridge and follow the Coastal Path along East Sands, past the Leisure Centre and up to the cliff top. Continue for about 1.5 miles, where the path descends to the shore; the Rock and Spindle is ahead. | **Tip** On your return, head for Jannetta's, a classic Italian gelateria and café that has been trading at 31 South Street for four generations, with 54 flavours of excellent home-made ice cream (Mon–Sat 9am–10pm, Sun 10am–10pm).

85 Saint Andrew
Scotland's X-man

Today it's the golf that draws the crowds to St Andrews, but in the Middle Ages the town's massive visitor appeal was all down to a miracle-working shrine containing a smattering of bones believed to be those of the apostle Andrew.

Known as the Morbrac (Gaelic for 'big speckled thing') it weighed a third of a ton, though the remains themselves amounted to just three fingers, an arm bone, a kneecap and a tooth. Quite how and when the supposed residue of the saint ended up here is unclear; the medieval relics trade was a murky business. There's the fable of St Rule, a 4th-century Greek monk inspired to take them to the ends of the earth (he didn't *quite* get there), and a more plausible tale that they were brought in AD 732 by the fugitive Bishop Acca of Northumberland. Either way, it was a tremendous coup for the settlement formerly known as Kilrymont, and ultimately for the whole country when, after a long contest for supremacy with St Columba, Andrew was affirmed in the 1320 Declaration of Arbroath as holy protector of Scotland. The nation could now boast as its patron saint no less a figure than the disciple first called by Christ. In later decades, the legend grew up that his death by crucifixion had taken place on an X-shaped cross, and this powerful totem, linked to the Greek letter that symbolised Christ, was soon officially adopted for the boldly distinctive Scottish flag, the saltire.

High on the turret of the Victorian town hall is a fine civic coat of arms showing the saint with limbs splayed to form a triumphant X; anyone unfamiliar with the story of his martyrdom might innocently think that he was jumping for joy. Standing in a niche across the road is a small but authoritative statue of Andrew that gives a hint of how the medieval town must have looked, though in fact it forms part of the 1920s remodelling of the *Citizen* newspaper offices in splendid Arts and Crafts style.

Address Photo 1: Town Hall, Queen's Gardens, KY16 9TA; Photo 2: J & G Innes, 107 South Steet, KY16 9QW | Getting there Bus to St Andrews; the two sculptures are in the town centre, a minute's walk from each other | Tip An over-life-sized statue of the saint in baroque style, by 19th-century sculptor Sir John Steell, stands in the garden of the university museum at 7 The Scores, which reopened in June 2021 after a major refurbishment. Now named the Wardlaw, the museum houses four thematic galleries showcasing its remarkable collections, plus changing exhibitions, and boasts splendid views from its open-air terrace (Mon–Fri 11am–7pm, Sat & Sun 10am–5pm).

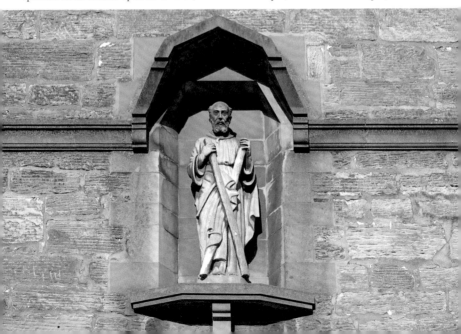

86 St Mary's College
In the beginning was the word

The unique street plan of St Andrews is due to the astute thinking of a long series of medieval bishops, who planned the wide thoroughfares for pilgrims converging on the cathedral, and subsequently filled the ancient burgh with seats of learning. The first university in Scotland (and the third in Britain) was founded here in 1413 by Bishop Henry Wardlaw. Like its predecessors in Oxford and Cambridge, it's based on a system of colleges, each with its own buildings, both teaching and residential. These are situated within the town but effectively set apart from it, with entrance gateways on the streets leading into enclosed courtyards and a network of connecting alleyways, creating a townscape unparalleled in Scotland.

St Mary's College, the third to be endowed, was founded in 1539 by Archbishop James Beaton, as New College. Devoted to the study of divinity, it's still ranked among the top 20 theology faculties worldwide. You pass through the gate under an appropriate motto from St John's gospel, *In principio erat verbum* ('In the beginning was the word'), and a coat of arms with, at its centre, an open book and a lily symbolising the Virgin Mary.

Dominating the picturesque green space within is a magnificent holm oak, well over 250 years old; a famous hawthorn tree, said to have been planted in the 1560s by Mary, Queen of Scots, is now rather frail, and keeps a lower profile. The spacious quadrangle is formed by buildings whose façades look substantially as they would have done when the college first opened its doors. On the street side is the fine King James Library, above the hall where the Scots parliament sat in 1645. It was in this upper chamber that pioneering mathematician James Gregory studied in the 17th century; his work in defining the first meridian (a very long time before the one at Greenwich was drawn) is commemorated in a line set into the floor, which is continued on the pavement of the street outside.

Address South Street, St Andrews, KY16 9JU | **Getting there** Bus to St Andrews | **Hours** Quadrangle open daily; King James Library, university term time, Mon–Fri 9am–5pm | **Tip** The independent Topping & Company Booksellers offers a delightful customer experience in a relaxed environment that sets it apart from the average bookshop. The bright, beautifully furnished store is extremely well stocked, with over 45,000 titles, and staff are enthusiastic and knowledgeable. Talks and readings are held regularly (7 Greyfriars Gardens, KY16 9HG, +44 (0)1334 585111, daily 9am–8.30pm).

87 __ St Rule's Tower

A coign of vantage with a kindly ghost

The squarely solid remains of St Rule's Church soar above the precinct of St Andrews Cathedral, at a discreet remove from the gaunt, fang-like wreck that was once the centre of the Scottish Church, and by far the largest cathedral ever built in the country. Though St Rule's is much the earliest building within the complex (and indeed the whole town), it has fared a great deal better over the years than its grandiose companion. From a distance, its immutable tower stands out like a staunch sentinel meerkat, impassively surveying the ruinous domain, now given over to a picturesque graveyard.

It was the fiery preaching of John Knox against the corrupt Catholic clergy that finally did for the cathedral, thus fuelling the orchestrated popular rebellion that brought about the Scottish Reformation. On 15 June, 1559, a furious mob smashed and ransacked the vast, splendid pile, whose construction had occupied two and a half centuries. The ambitious building had in fact suffered many previous ravages, both before and after its consecration in 1318, due to fires and storms, all the more destructive in its exposed coastal situation.

The tower of St Rule, on the other hand, has now stood tall for around 900 years, an emphatic tribute to the skill of the early medieval masons who built it. The church originally served the Augustinian priory established by Bishop Robert that guarded the relics of St Andrew, which were claimed to have been brought to the shores of Fife in the 4th century by the legendary St Regulus, or Rule (see ch. 85). The 108-foot tower, which was originally crowned with a simple spire, would have served as a beacon to pilgrims coming from both land and sea. It is, of course, haunted: the ghost of a kindly monk is reported to have assisted visitors who have difficulty climbing the 156 steps of the narrow spiral staircase that leads to the parapet and its spectacular panoramic views. On a clear day you can see as far as Arbroath, up the coast beyond the Tay estuary.

Address St Andrews Cathedral, The Pends, St Andrews, KY16 9QL, +44 (0)1334 472563, www.historicenvironment.scot | Getting there Bus to St Andrews | Hours Daily Apr–Sept 9.30am–5.30pm, Oct–Mar 10am–4pm (3pm Dec & Jan). Entry from Cathedral Museum; advance booking essential | Tip The street known as The Pends takes its name from the 14th-century priory gateway, long roofless but still magnificent, just outside the precinct wall. Its original impact is hard to appreciate due to the 5-foot rise in the road level over the centuries – plus the fact that it's used by vehicular traffic.

88 West Sands

A pretty good run for their money

Chariots of Fire, the inspirational true story of two British sprinters competing in the 1924 Olympics, has a special place in the annals of film. Made on a shoestring budget of £3 million, it was the maverick winner of four awards including best picture at the 1981 Oscars, prompting screenwriter Colin Welland's proud declaration 'The British are coming!', which heralded a resurgence of UK cinema after the doldrums of the previous decade. Today it's remembered above all for the much-imitated slow-motion running sequence that forms the backdrop to the credits, enhanced by the pulsating riffs of Vangelis' score. It's a scene that has brought serendipitous fame to the location where it was shot, the lovely two-mile-long West Sands in St Andrews.

The action follows a group of keen young men jogging along the shore (from left to right – always the direction of cinematic heroes) while the wind whips up white horses on a choppy sea. Then, as the camera pans to show the instantly recognisable Old Course golf links, a voice-over identifies the town as 'Broadstairs, Kent'. Cue hoots of incredulous derision from audiences all over Scotland.

The choice of location was led by economic considerations. Other scenes were set in Edinburgh and near Crieff, so it was practical to find a Scottish substitute for this short key sequence. But the shoot was far from problem-free. The original footage was filmed on a dull and windless day; however, a grain of sand in the camera was found to have spoiled the negative, which allowed the filmmakers to claim an extra day's shooting on their insurance. It was reshot a week later, on 1 May, 1980, when the weather was brighter though distinctly chilly. The camera tracks kept sinking into the sand, and leading actor Ben Cross later recalled the 'hell' of splashing through the surf and freezing water in the repeated takes.

A beach race is now held annually in which hundreds of runners recreate the experience – to the strains of Vangelis, naturally.

Address West Sands, St Andrews, KY16 9XL | **Getting there** Bus to St Andrews Bus Station | **Tip** For those seeking a real adrenaline rush by the sea, Blown Away is a mobile outdoor experience company based at West Sands that offers landyachting, surfing, stand-up paddle-boarding and other organised activities to individuals and groups. Tuition and safety gear are provided (+44 (0)7784 121125, www.blownaway.co.uk).

89 The Auld Kirk
An exquisite cliffhanger

St Monans' kirk sits calmly on the western margin of the parish, just yards from the edge of a cliff. This little gem of architecture has many distinctions: not only is it said to be the closest to the sea of all Scottish churches, it's also one of the oldest in the country that's still in use. In addition, it's one of the most recognisable, an unmistakable landmark on the East Neuk coast with its low octagonal spire and squat tower – and it's surely among the loveliest, reminiscent of a Cubist artwork in the subtle interrelationship of its planar forms. Its unusual T-plan (an intended nave was never built) is enhanced by the uplifting white interior, which is graced by features such as a 14th-century sedilia (decorative seating for three clerics) built into the south wall, and an 18th-century votive ship suspended in mid-air.

The first building on the site was a shrine to the saint who gave his name to the village. There is some doubt as to his true identity, but it seems probable that Monan, or Monanus, was an Irish missionary of the 9th century based on the Isle of May. The current Auld Kirk was built in the 1360s as a donation of King David II, supposedly in fulfilment of a vow, though again no one is certain of the details. The coherent appearance of the church is remarkable in view of its chequered history. The first scheme of repair and reconstruction came after it was torched by English invaders in 1544. Then, in the late 1820s, a renovation project under the direction of William Burn made considerable alterations to the interior. These were, however, reversed in the late 1950s as part of a sensitive restoration project, funded by a generous legacy.

The church's close proximity to the shore, which has increased over the centuries, seems entirely appropriate. The graveyard that surrounds the Auld Kirk speaks silent volumes about the history of a village where the livelihood of so many souls depended on the sea, and the precarious business of fishing.

Address Burnside, St Monans, KY10 2BX, www.stmonanschurch.org.uk | Getting there Bus 95 or X60 to St Monans | Hours Apr–Oct, daily 9am–5pm | Tip From the sublime to the gorblimey: the Welly Boot Garden of St Monans is just what its endearing name suggests – a colourful container garden of over 200 plant-filled wellies, created as a community initiative on the old harbour slipway. The sturdy rubber footwear, named after the Duke of Wellington, has a special place in British culture that can baffle foreigners.

90__Bowhouse
The local market that's got it all covered

The fields and waters of Fife teem with a vast cornucopia of comestibles, but the bulk of the harvest never makes it to local food outlets. Whether shellfish or soft fruit, wheat, meat or greens, most of the produce is transported straight to distant large-scale processors. This is a frustration that can irk visitors to the Kingdom almost as much as local residents and restaurateurs. But despite the continuing stranglehold of supermarkets and food service distributors, encouraging initiatives have emerged in recent years to increase awareness and availability of Fife's fresh fare, by linking growers and producers directly with the public.

The Bowhouse project is the brainchild of Toby Anstruther, who became involved in the promotion of local food businesses soon after taking over his ancestral family estate of Balcaskie. Initially, he developed farm steadings and plots for lease to small-scale producers, creating an environment where they could grow (in every sense), transform raw ingredients and sell their products in person to consumers. Then, borrowing a concept common in urban centres – the all-weather, covered space filled with individual stallholders – he transplanted it to the countryside, converting a modern barn as a base for markets and events, which began in 2017.

Several small artisan producers are housed in permanent units: there's a flour mill established by bread-making legend Andrew Whitley, who grows traditional, nutrient-rich varieties of wheat in fields on the estate, as well as an organic brewery and a well-known local butcher. Much of the produce on sale could hardly be fresher: plots just yards away house an agroecological market garden, and a flower farmer whose wares reflect the changing seasons. Other stallholders come from all over Fife and beyond with a wide range of food, drink and crafts; there's a family-friendly atmosphere, with street food, activities and live music in an adjoining hall.

Address Bowhouse Farm, St Monans, KY10 2DB, +44 (0)1333 720200, www.bowhousefife.com | **Getting there** On A 917, just west of St Monans, bus 95 or X60 to Bowhouse (request stop) | **Hours** Monthly, Sat & Sun 10am–4pm; see website for dates | **Tip** Each summer, Bowhouse is transformed into a venue for classical music during the East Neuk Festival; stacked wooden vegetable crates give a warm resonance to the acoustic. Known for its relaxed atmosphere, this exceptional 5-day festival features world-class musicians playing in a variety of halls and village churches (www.eastneukfestival.com).

91 East Pier Smokehouse
A refreshingly different kettle of fish

The A 917 coast road bypasses St Monans, giving the village an air of quiet self-containment and underlining its intense relationship with the sea. Fishing and boatbuilding were the mainstays of life here for centuries, and the focal point remains the harbour, with its long piers and breakwater that zigzags dramatically into the Firth of Forth. Preserving the freshness of the fishermen's catch was always a concern; one traditional method was smoking, and it's still highly valued locally for the flavour that it imparts, particularly to haddock, though spoilage has long ceased to be an issue.

When James Robb bought the harbourside building in 2005, the East Pier Smokehouse was an old fish-processing plant. Its transformation into a modern smoking facility and immaculately designed restaurant was a labour of love for the chef, who had made his reputation in Edinburgh as a much sought-after contract caterer. James' personal range of smoked fish goes way beyond the familiar varieties: hot-smoked whole sea bass is a favourite of regular diners, as are his smoked prawn tempura, crab cakes and langoustines. Smoked butter with garlic and herbs is an ingredient of several dishes, giving an extra kick to the Cullen skink soup and the tasty pan-fried sardines. There are always vegetarian options, featuring unusual smoked cheeses.

It's all excellent-value fare, based on quality local ingredients prepared with skill and care, inventively combined, but totally lacking in pretension and pointless flourishes. Meals are cooked to order and served in cardboard containers; they can be eaten in the dining room, on the upper terrace or under cover on the pier. Wherever you choose, you'll have an enviable sea view.

Visitors from over the border (or 'down south', as we Scots say) often rhapsodise about its similarity to Cornwall in the old days, though James's inspirations for the informal style came in fact from New Mexico and across the firth in North Berwick.

Address East Shore, St Monans, KY10 2AR, +44 (0)1333 405030/+44 (0)7432 279815, www.eastpier.co.uk | Getting there Bus 95 or X60 to St Monans | Hours Easter–Oct, Wed–Sun noon–2.30pm, Fri–Sun also 5–7.30pm | Tip The Jim Matthew Camera Collection comprises an astonishing array of over 3000 pieces of photographic equipment, from early Kodak Box Brownies to Soviet era Russian Photosnipers. Housed in the village's former Salvation Army Hall, it can currently be seen on occasional open days or by prior arrangement. A fundraising campaign is under way to enable its transformation into a visitor attraction (www.facebook.com/jmcameratrust).

92 The Windmill
Toiling at the pans

The concept of harnessing the wind as a source of energy goes back a long way in human history – the ranks of behemothic turbines that blight so many landscapes today are just its latest manifestation. In contrast, the lazy stone windmills of times gone by seem charmingly quaint, redolent of an era of bucolic bliss. However, the last remaining windmill in Fife bears witness to a very different story. The green surroundings, open sea views and rocky shore make the restored tower an idyllic spot to visit nowadays. But for half a century following its construction in 1772, the St Monans windmill was part of a grimy industrial site that belched clouds of smoke and steam by both day and night: the St Philips saltworks.

The complex was the property of Sir John Anstruther (see ch. 70), who reopened old coal workings and had them drained with steam pumps in order to exploit their low-grade fuel. This was used to fire nine panhouses on the shore, where salt was produced through evaporation, by boiling seawater in large metal pans. A wooden waggonway was constructed to connect the mines with the saltworks, and to carry the product on to Pittenweem harbour. The purpose of the windmill was to pump seawater uphill to a holding tank, through wooden pipes in a rock-cut channel.

Salt was a valuable commodity at the time, used as a preservative by the fishing industry, and for meat like salt beef, the staple of the British army in their colonial campaigns. Its manufacture was a highly profitable enterprise for the aristocratic pit owners, who kept miners and salters in a state of serfdom until reforms in the 1790s. As the fires had to be tended round the clock, cottages were sited next to the panhouses, and women and children were also employed in back-breaking work. The St Monans works have now been reclaimed by nature, and designated a Site of Special Scientific Interest. It hosts a variety of seabird and crustacean species.

Address Coal Farm, St Monans, KY10 2DQ | Getting there Bus 95 or X60 to St Monans; the site is just east of the village, along the coastal path | Hours Currently viewable from the outside only. Check www.onfife.com for information on access to the interior, provided by Coastwatch St Monans. | Tip The red-stained rocks along the shore get their colour from the iron salts in what's known as a chalybeate spring. In the 17th century this water, which emerged in St Monans at a well on East Braes, was famed for its health-giving properties.

93 Bishop's Wood

Rough justice for Sharp practice

Just south of Strathkinness is an attractive community woodland, a pleasant spot for a peaceful stroll that conceals a sombre reminder of a much darker past. The path, through stands of native birch and thickets swathed in honeysuckle, partially follows the route of the ancient road to St Andrews, over what was once the bleak wasteland of Magus Muir – the site of the notorious murder, on 3 May, 1679, of Scotland's leading churchman, Archbishop James Sharp.

This was a time of fervid and violent religious turmoil. Sharp was a deeply unpopular figure, a wheeler-dealer in church politics whose loyalties had shifted from Presbyterianism to Anglicanism and who then actively pursued the persecution of his former confederates, the Covenanters. However, it was pure chance that brought about his grisly demise on that day.

The archbishop was making a leisurely return from Edinburgh to St Andrews with his daughter Isabel, travelling in a state coach with an entourage of servants. The party had made a last stop at Ceres, where Sharp enjoyed a smoke and a drink with the minister, and were on the homeward stretch across the expanse of Magus Muir when they were overtaken by a band of nine horsemen – zealous Covenanters with pistols and swords. Their intended target was in fact the Sheriff of Fife, who was suppressing local religious gatherings at open-air assemblies known as conventicles, but the men took the chance encounter as a sign of divine intervention. After shooting at the hapless prelate, they dragged him from his coach and hacked him to death. It was, incidentally, the day before his 66th birthday.

Some 200 years after the event, a red sandstone cairn in the form of a rustic pyramid was erected as a memorial by local landowner John Whyte-Melville. In a field just outside the wood are the graves of five Covenanters who were hanged in retribution, although they played no part in the killing.

Address Bishop's Wood, Strathkinness, KY16 9RZ | **Getting there** Buses 42A or 64 to Strathkinness (Danskin Place), then walk south down Main Street; the wood is beyond the village on the right. The Archbishop's monument is in the north-west, along a clearly marked path; the Covenanters' graves are in an enclosure in a nearby field, just beyond the trees. | **Tip** The Tavern at Strathkinness is a popular family-run pub with a menu featuring locally sourced produce (www.strathkinnesstavern.co.uk, Mon–Thu from 5pm, Fri–Sun from noon).

94___The Cold War Bunker
Not with a bang but a whimper

There's a rather comical irony in the marketing of 'Scotland's best-kept secret' – a hidden nuclear bunker decommissioned in 1993 that's now a well-publicised visitor attraction, with conspicuous signposts to guide you to its location. But the place itself is definitely no laughing matter. Ominous military hardware flanks the oddly porticoed bungalow at the entrance. Supposed to pass as a normal Fife farmhouse, this was built to disguise the access to a labyrinth over 130 feet underground – a massive double-storey complex of operations rooms, service areas and living quarters, encased in a 10-foot thick concrete shell, reinforced at 6-inch intervals with 1-inch tungsten rods. Designed in 1951 as a radar station, it was later repurposed as a regional headquarters from where the armed forces would have run the country, or what was left of it, in the event of nuclear war. The electrical plant, air filtration and food supplies were capable of sustaining 300 personnel for three months in what would surely have been a kind of desperate purgatory.

Now reconstructed with original equipment from the Cold War era, the bunker has a strange familiarity to those brought up on the celluloid spy fiction of the 1960s. Quirkily British details catch the eye: lime green nylon seat covers, cigars on the Minister of State's desk, a cat flap on a high-security door. But though you might meet Cleo, the blue-eyed Bengal mouser with access to all areas, you may be sure that no hunky action hero in a black polo-neck is going to burst in and save the day.

Sobering statistics are on display to remind us that the world's nuclear arsenals still pose the threat of death and destruction on an unimaginable scale. It's an utterly absorbing experience – and you'll be so grateful to get out again. For those born since the dissolution of the USSR, however, the effect seems to be different. The bunker is rented out for parties, and even weddings in the fully furnished chapel: *carpe diem*, and all that!

Address Crown Buildings, Troywood, KY16 8QH, +44 (0)1333 310301, www.secretbunker.co.uk | Getting there On the B 9131 between St Andrews and Anstruther, take the B 940 east; bus X60 to B1931/B940 crossroads, then a 20-minute walk | Hours Feb–Nov, daily 10am–5pm (last admission) | Tip Be sure to visit the two bunker cinemas, where Peter Watkins' harrowing 1965 docudrama *The War Game* is shown alongside grimly risible public information films from the 1960s and '70s. There is also a café in the original, surprisingly small mess hall.

95 Sir Jimmy Shand
The toe-tapping Laird o' Muchty

Fife has a rich musical heritage that has produced talent in every genre from punk to opera. The burgh of Auchtermuchty alone has nurtured not only the defiantly Scots-accented rock duo The Proclaimers, but the greatest ever exponent of a very different popular tradition. In his heyday of the 1950s and '60s, the bright, crisp 'dunt' of accordionist Jimmy Shand and his band brought the strict tempo reels and jigs of Scottish country dance music to a huge public, becoming *the* definitive sound of Scotland for millions worldwide.

Jimmy's musical career began in earnest in the early 1930s, after his skills on the button accordion impressed a Dundee music shop proprietor; he was soon making his first 78s, and by the end of the decade he'd had an instrument built to his own specifications by the German firm Hohner. He made the first of countless radio broadcasts on New Year's Day 1945, and by the mid-1950s was releasing a new single every month, many of them his own compositions. His biggest hit, *The Bluebell Polka* – produced by the legendary George Martin – came on the cusp of a new musical era, entering the charts just weeks after Bill Haley's *Rock around the Clock*. The new medium of TV brought further fame; in 1964 his band even appeared on *Top of the Pops*. They were in constant demand all over the UK, and Jimmy's insistence on driving back home every night – even from the south of England – meant a gruelling lifestyle that many rock stars would have baulked at. There were also regular international tours, with capacity houses in major venues from Sydney Opera House to New York's Carnegie Hall.

Erected in 2003, David Annand's memorial statue captures the quiet authority of a modest master. Despite the adulation and honours bestowed on him, the man known fondly as the Laird o' Muchty did not relish the limelight, and declared towards the end of his long life that he was never meant to be an entertainer.

Address Upper Greens, Auchtermuchty, KY14 7BS | Getting there Bus 36, 64, 66/A, 94A to Auchtermuchty; the statue is signposted and is right next to a small car park | Tip Though always associated with 'Muchty', where he settled in 1957, Sir Jimmy never forgot his birthplace of East Wemyss. A memorial plaque can be found there on Main Street, near the foreshore, unveiled in 2008 to mark the centenary of his birth, and a street in the village is named Sir Jimmy Shand Court in his memory.

96 Balmerino Abbey

Commune of the white monks

If you've ever wondered what 'razed to the ground' means in practice, Balmerino Abbey is a good place to find out. It's a lovely, tranquil spot, on a terrace overlooking the Tay estuary, but without the aid of the interpretation panel and leaflets available on site, it would be hard to imagine the original scale and appearance of the buildings that stood here throughout the late Middle Ages. Nothing remains of the 206-foot-long abbey church and its glorious soaring vaults except the foundations and some sad fragments of wall. Somewhat better preserved are the atmospheric remnants of the chapter house and the monks' parlour, though these are now too dangerous to enter.

Balmerino was founded in 1229 by 12 monks from Melrose Abbey, at the invitation of Queen Ermengarde, widow of William I. She was later buried in front of the altar, at a site now marked by a simple wooden cross.

The monastery was part of a vast Europe-wide network established by the formidable Cistercian order, who prospered from their principle of living off the manual labour of the brotherhood. Known as the white monks due to their distinctive robes of undyed wool, they formed strictly disciplined, self-sufficient communities who farmed, fished and contributed greatly to the development of rural areas. Balmerino's decline began when an English army set fire to it in 1547, and continued 12 years later with its comprehensive pillaging by Reformation rabble. Around 1600, parts of the complex were converted into a private residence, ensuring their survival; the rest of the stonework was gradually carted away and reused elsewhere. A few ornamental elements were incorporated into an adjacent farm steading. An impressively gnarled and knotted Spanish chestnut tree stands nearby; planted in the mid-16th century, it's among the oldest trees in Scotland, and is traditionally associated with a visit to Balmerino by Mary, Queen of Scots.

Address Balmerino, DD6 8SB | Getting there Off B 946, 3.5 miles west of Wormit (signposted from A 92); to book Fife Council's Go Flexi taxibus service phone +44 (0)1382 540624 | Hours Unrestricted | Tip The remains of Balmerino pier can be seen on the nearby shore. Though it's hard to believe today, this was for centuries an important river crossing point and busy harbour, exporting flax, grain, lime and local fish, including the much-prized Tay sparling (also known as smelt), now rare in Scottish waters.

97 Scottish Deer Centre
Animal magic

Familiar to millions in the shape of Landseer's majestic *Monarch of the Glen*, the red deer has been an iconic symbol of Scotland since Victorian times. When the Scottish Deer Centre was first established over 30 years ago, it was a unique venture devoted solely to this native species, offering hands-on encounters as well as an appreciation of red deer biology, their historic association with humans and the health benefits of eating venison.

Since then, although the name hasn't changed, the 55-acre park has altered both its focus and scope, and in 2011 it became a fully accredited zoo. In addition to red deer, it currently houses 11 varieties from around the world, including the once-native reindeer, together with several other species of magnificent wildlife that used to roam freely over the Scottish countryside.

Wolves have now returned to the park, and visitors can also enjoy watching brown bears, common here until the end of the last Ice Age, as well as elk and lynx, both of which died out not much more than 1,000 years ago; many rewilding advocates would like to see them reintroduced. And if you're by their enclosure at feeding time, you're sure to get a sighting of the reclusive Scottish wildcat, now sadly all but extinct in the wild, thanks chiefly to hybridisation with domestic felines. Red squirrels populate the small woodland: you may catch a lucky glimpse from the tree-top walkway. But it's the numerous deer that are most popular among younger visitors, particularly the beautifully dappled fallow and sika, which flock to be fed from little hands (pelleted fodder can be bought at the entrance). The keepers and rangers give informative talks and tours, there are trailer rides through the fields, and you mustn't miss the falconry displays held in the grassy arena, with the thrilling opportunity for a close look at hawks, falcons and owls, and their different flying and hunting techniques.

Address Bow of Fife, KY15 4NQ, +44 (0)1337 810391 | Getting there Buses 42 or 64 to Scottish Deer Centre | Hours Daily 10am–4.30pm | Tip Fife Coast and Countryside Trust manages several reserves where wildlife can be spotted in a natural environment, including Birnie and Gaddon Lochs, 2.5 miles west along the A91 from the Deer Centre (and served by the same buses), where you'll find a great variety of bird life, as well as mammals including otters, bats and red squirrels.

98 Cupar Heritage Trail

The tantalising past of the old county town

The place name of Cupar – the Pictish word for 'confluence of two rivers' – is testament to the ancient origins of the settlement where the Lady Burn meets the River Eden. A large network of local routes converged at the crossings, and the old road from Edinburgh to Dundee passed through the town. In the Middle Ages, Cupar developed as a royal burgh and prosperous trading hub, at the very heart of Fife: it was the county town from 1214 until local government reorganisation in 1974. Apart from the old church tower, however, whose lower half dates from 1415, little remains of medieval Cupar except its general layout, and the townscape is now characterised chiefly by fine buildings from its 19th-century heyday.

A good way to see the highlights at your leisure is by following the well-interpreted heritage trail promoted by Cupar Development Trust. One striking feature is the impressive variety of spires, from the bold Gothic fantasy of the Duncan Institute to the soaring elegance of St John's Church, not to mention the slate-covered 'chimney steeple' atop St Columba's R.C. Church, a cute little cousin of Liverpool Metropolitan Cathedral. Another surprise is the imposing neoclassical façade of Watt's, built in 1814 as a remarkably grand prison, later occupied by a seed merchant and subsequently a popular restaurant and nightclub.

Probably the most tantalising spot is the motte that once housed the long-gone castle. After its destruction in the 14th century, the castle hill became an open space used for public entertainments, and in 1552 it was the site of the first complete performance of *A Satire of the Three Estates* by Sir David Lyndsay. A radical, witty and challenging attack on the governance of the country, this is the earliest example of Scottish drama whose full text survives. It was first revived at the 1948 Edinburgh Festival, and has recently been performed on its original 'stage' – now a car park.

Address The heritage trail map and leaflet can be downloaded at www.cupardevtrust.org; copies are also available at the Library on Crossgate. The places are marked by blue plaques. The site pictured is Castlehill Centre, KY15 4HA. | Getting there Train to Cupar; bus 41, 42, 64, X24, X54, X59 or X61 | Tip Cupar Heritage Centre is an excellent volunteer-run facility with changing exhibitions on local history themes (Cupar Railway Station, KY15 5HX, www.cuparheritage.org.uk, mid-Apr–Oct, Wed, Fri & Sun 2–4.30pm).

99 Hill of Tarvit

Upstairs, downstairs and out on the green

A trip to the country estate of Hill of Tarvit offers a fascinating perspective on a bygone style of life. The site was first occupied well over 2,000 years ago, but the era that today's visitors step back to is the early 20th-century heyday of a well-to-do family – recent times in chronological terms, though in some respects practically as remote as the Iron Age.

The house then known as Wemyss Hall, a 17th-century mansion with later extensions, was purchased in 1904 along with its large estate by Frederick Sharp, the scion of a Dundee jute-manufacturing family who had prospered as a financier. Sharp engaged the distinguished architect Robert Lorimer (see ch. 60) to make radical alterations to the building, with the dual aim of creating a comfortable family home and of showcasing his magnificent collection of antique furniture, paintings, tapestries and porcelain.

The result is a series of lofty, elegant interiors, each in a contrasting style that complements its contents, with exquisite detailing in everything from the ornamental plasterwork ceilings to the drawing room door handles. All 'mod cons' were installed (including Lorimer's patent lavatory, the Remirol), and the service wing was thoughtfully designed for the 12 live-in staff. Lorimer's brief extended to landscaping the 279-acre grounds, with formal enclosed gardens, green terracing and rolling parkland beyond.

Sharp was a keen golfer, and in 1924 he had his own nine-hole course, Kingarrock, laid out near the house. It was reinstated in 2008 following the original plan, and now, maintained by a score of sheep, it operates as a unique sporting venue – the only course in the UK played exclusively as it was when golf was still an art, using original hickory-shafted clubs and authentic mesh-pattern balls. The green fee includes equipment, tips from the experienced team and post-game refreshments; plus fours are optional.

Address Hill of Tarvit, Cupar, KY15 5PB, +44 (0)1334 653127, www.nts.org.uk; Kingarrock Hickory Golf: +44 (0)1334 653421, kingarrock@nts.org.uk | **Getting there** Bus 64 to end of drive and a 12-minute walk | **Hours** House: mid-Apr–Oct, Sat & Sun 11am–5pm; golf course: Mar–Oct, daily from 10am; garden and grounds: daily dawn–dusk | **Tip** There are several walks to be enjoyed within the lovely wooded grounds; details are on the website. The climb to the monument on 692-foot-high Wemyss Hill is steep, but well worth the effort for the panoramic views.

100 Scotstarvit Tower

Status symbol of a sardonic Scot

Fortified tower houses were a typical feature of the medieval Scottish landscape, and many examples survive today, often restored to a comfortably habitable condition. Generally reaching around four storeys, they're a comparatively basic kind of tall castle that began to become popular with the Scots gentry in the 14th century. Their design continued to evolve for 300 years, until social and economic changes made this kind of defensible residence obsolete.

Scotstarvit stands on a ridge just south of Cupar. It's a fine early 17th-century L-plan tower house, with some unorthodox aspects that derive from the unusual laird who had it built. Sir John Scot (1586 – 1670) was one of the most enterprising men of his time – a judge, politician and classics scholar who was also responsible for the publication of the first proper maps of Scotland. He acquired the estate then known as Inglis Tarvit in 1611; as a writer skilled in wordplay, it must have pleased him to alter the 'English' part of its name to Scots. Built on the site of a previous building, his tower house was completed in 1627 – the date on a monogrammed panel over the stairhead – but designed to look much older, giving it an ancestral gravitas and, perhaps, evoking nostalgia for Scotland's good old days. It has five storeys, plus an attic used as his private study. One odd feature is the absence of a kitchen; presumably this was housed in a lost outbuilding, since many of the great minds of the day were entertained at Scotstarvit.

Though in earlier life he was celebrated for his Latin verse, the work by which Sir John is now remembered was written in his 80th year. *The Staggering State of the Scots Statesmen* is a sardonic memoir reflecting on the fragility of success, inspired by his own fall from grace after decades of public service. Much later, the Victorian author Thomas Carlyle summed it up as 'a homily on life's nothingness, enforced by examples'.

Address Scotstarvit, near Cupar, KY15 5PA | **Getting there** Bus 64 to Hill of Tarvit and short walk down the lane (no cars allowed) opposite the entrance to Hill of Tarvit Mansion | **Hours** Apr–Sept, Sat & Sun 11am–5pm | **Tip** Mount Hill, three miles north-west of Cupar, is the site of the 100-foot high Hopetoun Monument, erected in 1826 and visible for miles around. Fit and brave individuals who want to climb the 172 unlit steps to the top can get the keys from West Hall Farm, KY15 4NA.

101 Eden Mill Distillery

The doctrine of original gin

Just a decade ago, gin was widely dismissed as a one-note drink, jokingly vilified as 'mother's ruin' and the province of a stuffy older generation. Its resurrection as a modish, nuanced premium spirit began in London in 2009, after a long campaign for the repeal of the 1751 Act that had outlawed small-scale distilleries. Scotland soon took up the torch, and the nation famed worldwide as the home of whisky now also produces 70 per cent of the UK's gin.

Fife's Eden Mill was established in 2014 within the former Guardbridge paper mill, on the extensive estuary of the River Eden. This earthly paradise for drinkers already had a history of alcohol production when co-founder Paul Miller set up his original micro-brewery here in 2012. From 1810 to 1860 the site had been the home of the legendary Haig Brothers' grain whisky distillery, and this motivated the Eden team's expansion from wood-matured beers into spirits. They began with whisky, reviving interest in the skill of blend-ing before launching their own estimable single malt in 2018.

But it was their venture into small-batch gin production that really caught the contemporary *zeitgeist*. Besides the core ingredient of juniper berries, Eden Mill's unique portfolio is subtly blended with flavourings including hops (a natural choice for brewers) and select botanicals, many of which, like the vitamin-C-rich sea buckthorn, are sourced locally. All are bottled in stoneware flasks, originally intended for premium beer and cleverly repurposed as part of the gin's distinctive identity. Eden Mill's success is such that they are currently expanding their premises, creating a larger distillery and brewery within the mill building to allow for increased production and new visitor facilities. The thorough refurbishment will include that of the mill clock, an iconic symbol of the village, which has sur-vived both a wartime bombing raid and the more recent theft of its mechanism (since recovered).

Address Main Street, Guardbridge, KY16 0US, +44 (0)1334 834038, www.edenmill.com |
Getting there Bus 42, 59, 92/A/B/C/D, 94 or 99/A/B to Guardbridge | Hours While the
expansion is underway, tutored tastings of gin, whisky and beer are held in the Gatehouse
visitor centre, opposite the mill clock (book via website) | Tip Just across the old bridge is
Malcolm Antiques, an eclectic complex with a café and sunny terrace on the river. Keen bird-
watchers should seek out the hide overlooking Eden Estuary Nature Reserve (signposted off
Main Street; daily 9am – 5pm (4pm Nov – Mar); for access code phone +44 (0)7985 707593).

102 St Athernase Church

The discreet charm of the Romanesque

Most people who know the name of Leuchars associate it with just two things: the Royal Air Force base that it hosted for almost a century, and its railway station – the nearest to St Andrews since the draconian closure of the branch line to the university town and golf mecca in 1969. But if you choose to take the short walk from the station into the little town itself, rather than a bus or taxi for 'onward travel', you will discover a rare architectural gem of a character and charm unparalleled in Scotland.

Standing high on a grassy knoll in confident serenity, as befits what is still very much a working church, St Athernase is witness to over 800 years of change. The building as we see it today is a composite affair, begun around 1150 but much altered and extended: the cute pepper-pot bell turret was added in 1745, and the simple nave in 1857. Nonetheless, the survival of the exquisite 12th-century chancel and apse is enough for the church to be acclaimed as one of the finest examples of the Romanesque ecclesiastical style in the UK. This revolution in architecture, characterised by masonry vaulting, semi-circular arches and a massive yet capacious solidity, was a hugely significant element of 'what the Normans did for us'. Robert de Quinci was the local Anglo-Norman baron responsible for the main phase of construction at Leuchars; he also built a substantial castle to the north, now long gone.

The exterior of the east end is a stunning sight, dominated by ornately carved decorative arcading and intersecting arches. The corbels above are embellished with grotesque carved stone heads, a feature of Romanesque art that harks back to the pagan past, then not far distant. The equivalent section of the interior is much plainer – it would originally have been painted – but it remains a compelling space that preserves a timeless quality of restorative calm and solace.

A stroll round the churchyard is also highly recommended.

Address 14 Main Street, Leuchars, KY16 0HN, +44 (0)1334 870038 | Getting there
Train to Leuchars, then walk north-east up Station Road and right at the junction with
Main Street | Hours Apr–Oct, daily 10am–4pm approx.; guided tours July & Aug,
Tue 10am–noon & 2–4pm; church service all year Sun 11am | Tip Nearby Earlshall
Castle is a picture-perfect 16th/17th-century mansion, restored in the 1890s by Robert
Lorimer, with extensive gardens including a glorious topiary lawn. It's privately owned,
but the grounds are open occasionally (see www.scotlandsgardens.org).

103 The Orchard Town

The fruits of an ancient heritage

Like so many other British towns accorded the same prefix in days of yore, Newburgh is in fact an old settlement. It grew up in the 13th century just west of the abbey of Lindores, founded in 1191 by the Tironensian Order, a French Celtic offshoot of the Benedictines. The monks lived by manual labour: known for their building skills, they were also innovative agriculturalists. Though Lindores now lies in ruin, the community's other legacy to the area – fruit tree cultivation – has proved much more lasting.

At one time the abbey's orchards extended for over 30 acres, along the hillside now occupied by the town. The French monks brought with them not only know-how, but a new species of fruit: it was they who introduced the first pears to Scotland, a hard, starchy, storable variety, handy for soup in that pre-potato era. The brothers' produce was destined for trade as well as for their own consumption; they were also pioneering distillers, making fruit-flavoured *aqua vitae* which they supplied to the royal court at Falkland.

The abbey was sacked in the Reformation, but Newburgh's orchards lived on, as long strips of private garden hidden behind the façades of High Street houses. Their crops of plums, pears and apples became widely famed when the town developed as a tourist destination in the 19th century, and up to the 1960s amateur growers still sold fruit at their doors. In 2002, the Newburgh Orchard Group was formed by local people keen to maintain and develop this now threatened heritage, and two years later, a community orchard was planted by local primary school pupils. Newburgh has since been hailed, in a survey for the Orchard Revival movement, as 'perhaps Scotland's finest fruit town', with a total of over 1,000 mostly mature trees, including rare old varieties. The annual harvest is celebrated at the group's autumn markets in the High Street. Get there early for the best choice – they sell out rapidly!

Address Community Orchard: off Cupar Road, Newburgh, KY14 6HA (entrance at car park next to Newburgh Primary School), www.newburghorchards.org.uk | Getting there Bus 36 to Newburgh | Hours Fruit markets, Aug–Oct, Sat, 9.30am–12.30pm; check website for details of these and other Orchard Group activities | Tip Lindores is now home to a distillery, where the ancient monastic craft was revived in 2017. Their first single malt whisky, released in 2021, has already won a prestigious award, and they also make a spicy, herby *aqua vitae*. Tours of the historic site are available (www.lindoresabbeydistillery.com).

104_ The Unknown Bairn

Unnamed, but not unmourned

Just over half a century ago, the quiet community of Tayport was shaken by a strange and distressing mystery that haunts the town to this day. It was a Sunday afternoon in May 1971, and local postman Ian Robertson was taking his five-year-old son Neil for a walk along the beach when he spotted what looked like a large doll lying where it had been washed up by the tide. It turned out to be a harrowing discovery: the body of a boy aged about three, which had clearly been in the water for some time.

A pathologist confirmed that he had died of natural causes, and it was assumed that police enquiries would soon lead to his identification. But no child matching his description had been reported missing, and despite a nationwide appeal for information and massive media coverage, no one ever came forward to solve the mystery of who he was or where he was from. Speculation that he had been on a vessel lost at sea came to nothing; in fact it transpired that his death, though not suspicious, was probably not due to drowning. Years later, detectives involved in the investigation revealed that the most likely explanation was that his parents were tinkers or travellers, living on the margins of society, too poor to pay for a funeral when their infant son died of natural causes, and subsequently too intimidated to come forward with all the publicity surrounding the case.

The child forever remembered as the unknown bairn was buried in Tayport cemetery, near the shores where he was found, with a headstone paid for by donations from all over the country. Flowers and toys are still left there by the local community. The Robertsons were deeply affected by their role in the poignant story, tending the grave and leading the mourning each year on the anniversary of his discovery. Sadly, Ian and Neil have both now passed away; they are laid to rest just a few feet away from the nameless child that Ian always thought of as part of the family.

Address Tayport Cemetery, Newport Road, Tayport, DD6 9AU, +44 (0)1334 659336 | Getting there Bus 42, 70 or 92 to Tayport Cemetery; the grave is near the north-east corner | Hours Unrestricted | Tip The Harbour Café in Tayport is a welcoming community-run venture on the waterfront, with views across the Tay to Broughty Ferry Castle (10 Broad Street, DD6 9AJ, daily till 4pm). In the heart of the town on Whitenhill, look out for the leaning clock tower of the Auld Kirk, now an exhibition and concert venue.

105__ The Polish Camp

The eagle and the lion

Tentsmuir is an invigorating expanse of coastal terrain at the north-eastern tip of Fife, with beaches, dunes, pine forest and heathland. Offshore, the mighty River Tay rushes to meet the North Sea; as currents clash, vast quantities of sediment are deposited, creating constantly shifting sandbanks. Parts of the area are a nature reserve, where fauna from seals and seabirds to roe deer and red squirrels may be spotted. Humans were living here by 7,000 BC, when the coastline lay further inland; tools and arrowheads of the Mesolithic Era have been found near Morton Lochs, on what was probably then a tidal island. All that came to an end around 5,000 BC, when a massive tsunami travelled across from the Norwegian coast, with catastrophic results. Much later, the same route brought another wave of change in the person of emigrant Viking farmers, drawn by the land's rich resources to settle here.

Fast forward to 1940, and Tentsmuir was once again under threat from Norway, then occupied by the Nazis. The long sandy beaches and shallow waters made it an ideal site for the anticipated German invasion, and the air base at nearby Leuchars was a likely target for a seaborne attack. The protection of this coast became a matter of urgency, and the work of building and operating defences was entrusted to units of the Polish Army, relocated to Scotland after the fall of their nation. Stretches of the anti-tank concrete blocks that were placed at the high-water line can still be seen, now far inland.

Other wartime traces survive among the trees that have grown up since, notably a roofless brick building with two fireplaces, once part of an encampment which the Polish soldiers constructed and then lived in. A few yards from it is a well with a poignant coat of arms on one side, deftly drawn in wet cement. It shows the eagle insignia that the Poles wore on their berets, alongside the lion rampant of Scotland, with a defiant thistle below.

Address Polish Camp Road, Tentsmuir Forest, KY16 0DR | Getting there From B945, take road to Kinshaldy Beach. Alternatively, follow Fife Coastal Path from Leuchars. Polish Camp Road leads north into the woods off the Kinshaldy road. The site is across a narrow bridge over a ditch, at OS map reference NO 480 240 | Hours Unrestricted | Tip The small mosaic on the exterior of St Andrews Town Hall is a colourful memorial to the contribution of the Polish Army during WWII. Created by three Polish servicemen and unveiled in 1941, it shows a Polish soldier sustained by Scotland's patron saint.

106__ The Tay Bridge Disaster
'Remember'd for a very long time'

The original iron bridge that carried the railway across the Firth of Tay, linking Fife to Dundee, was opened on 31 May, 1878 to huge acclaim. With 85 spans, it measured nearly two miles, making it the longest bridge in the world. Queen Victoria crossed in the royal train shortly afterwards, before knighting its designer, Thomas Bouch. But just 19 months later disaster struck, when the central section collapsed 'like matchwood' during a fierce gale, taking with it a train and six carriages full of passengers. There were no survivors. Though speculation about the cause continues to this day, the official enquiry laid the blame squarely on Bouch's failure to provide the bridge with sufficient bracing against the wind.

There is dark irony in the fact that the best-known account of this tragic event is the unintentionally humorous doggerel of *The Tay Bridge Disaster*, the work of 'giftedly bad' Dundee poet William Topaz McGonagall. After a nod to the 'silv'ry Tay' comes his oft-quoted lament: 'Alas! I am very sorry to say/That ninety lives have been taken away/On the last Sabbath day of 1879/Which will be remember'd for a very long time'.

A grim physical reminder of the disaster still remains: the stumps of the original piers, visible at low tide next to the replacement bridge. But McGonagall's well-meaning verses were essentially its chief memorial until the 134th anniversary in 2013, when two simple, poignant monuments, one on either side of the firth, were unveiled by descendants of two of the crew who perished. The identical trios of eight-foot granite slabs, in Wormit and across the water in Dundee, are inscribed with the names and ages of the 59 known victims. The number was wrongly reported at the time as 75, due to a miscalculation of tickets sold. No one knows why McGonagall's poem quotes the figure of 90 – it surely wasn't to help with scansion, a concept quite alien to him.

Address Wormit Bay, DD6 8LX | **Getting there** Bus 70, 77/A/B or 92/A to Riverside Road, then walk down Bay Road, under the railway bridge and continue when the road becomes a surfaced path along the foreshore | **Tip** The award-winning Newport Restaurant is two miles east along the coast in the Victorian town of Newport-on-Tay, from where steamboat ferries known as Fifies once plied the firth. It boasts a two-storey glass wall offering westerly vistas of the distant rail bridge (1 High Street, Newport-on-Tay, DD6 8AB, www.thenewportrestaurant.co.uk; rooms also available).

107 The Artline
Platforms for creativity

The train journey through Fife on the Edinburgh – Dundee mainline could justifiably be classed as an artistic event. It begins the moment that the massive rail bridge conducts you high above the shimmering expanse of the Forth; then come sublime vistas of rocky shores and endless sands, spiced with diverse treats – distant islands, basking seals, an intriguing scrapyard. Add in a handful of charming Victorian stations, and it's a true visual feast.

What's more, almost everywhere that the train stops there is cultural endeavour to be found on the spot: thanks to an imaginative station adoption scheme, a variety of artists and heritage enthusiasts have in recent years developed new uses for an assortment of fine railway buildings, now surplus to operational requirements.

Kirsty Lorenz was the first to bring artistry to the tracks, when in 2009 she converted the disused restaurant on platform 2 at Ladybank into studio space for her joyous flower paintings. Shortly thereafter the old stationmaster's house at Kinghorn was transformed into a gallery and studios by a gifted duo, watercolourist and teacher Lynette Gray, who runs regular art classes, and her painter-printmaker husband Douglas. Both take inspiration from aspects of the local surroundings for their engaging and thought-provoking images – with delightfully contrasting results.

Heritage centres and more studios soon sprang up in and around stations from North Queensferry to Cupar. Ladybank's splendid Off the Rails Arthouse was set up by a lively collective as a hub for art and design projects, and the enterprising Lynette went on to establish a second base in the signal box at Aberdour's enchanting station, where she creates graceful ceramic birds. It's also to her credit that the Artline group was formed in 2015, hosting annual showcases of art and heritage involving up to 11 station venues, at open weekends featuring poetry, music and practical demonstrations.

Address Stations from North Queensferry to Cupar; www.theartline.co.uk. Photo 1: Aberdour Station, KY3 0SN; Photo 2: Ladybank Station House, KY15 7JT | **Getting there** Train; an off-peak day return ticket allows you to break your journey *en route* | **Hours** Though the Artline open weekends are not being run at present, several venues are open regularly to the public and others are visitable by appointment; see website for details | **Tip** Many of Fife's professional artists, makers and designers participate in open studio weekends: see www.centralfifeopenstudios.org, www.eastneukopenstudios.org and www.openstudiosfife.co.uk (which covers North Fife).

108 The Coastal Path

Walking the fringe of gold

Though it was probably coined by an earlier king, the description of Fife as 'a beggar's mantle fringed with gold lace' is generally attributed to James VI. Regardless of the regal wordsmith responsible, it's a vivid metaphor, comparing the poor, boggy land of the interior with the prosperous trading ports round the coast.

But the phrase also resonates down the ages as an evocation of the coastline's timeless natural glory. The golden strands and rugged rocks that swathe the peninsula's shores get more annual sunshine than most of the UK, and the luminosity of the maritime air lends them their own particular glow.

Since 2002 it has been easy to explore this stunning shoreline on foot, thanks to the Fife Coastal Path, a well-managed trail that guides walkers along its diverse terrain and contrasting features, natural and man-made, rural and urban, from ancient to post-industrial. The path originally began and ended at the bridges over the firths of Forth and Tay, but it has since been extended at each end to take in the upper reaches of the two estuaries, and now runs from Kincardine in the south to Newburgh in the north. Walkers who aim to complete the entire 117-mile route – Scotland's longest continuous coastal footpath – generally do it in eight day-long sections; many prefer the anti-clockwise direction, which keeps the prevailing wind at their back for most of the way.

There are over 50 'welcome ports' *en route*, offering practical information on eating places, toilets and public transport as well as details of local places of interest: a significant number of the sites in this book are in fact within striking distance of the path. The Harbourmaster's House at Dysart (see ch. 47) is the headquarters of the Fife Coast and Countryside Trust, the environmental charity which manages the path. It has an excellent interactive exhibition that offers insights into many aspects of the route, including its rich biodiversity.

Address The path runs from Kincardine to Newburgh; the photo shows the gateway that marks the Newburgh end. See www.fifecoastandcountrysidetrust.co.uk for full details of the route. | **Getting there** Buses serve Kincardine, Newburgh and numerous places *en route* | **Tip** The Kingdom of Fife Millennium Cycle Ways are perfect for those who prefer to take their recreation on two wheels. One of the UK's most comprehensive networks for cyclists, they offer over 300 miles of safe and signposted routes, including a 105-mile round trip between the Forth and Tay road bridges (www. fifedirect.org.uk/fife-cycleways).

109_ The Little Houses
New homes for old

Mention the National Trust for Scotland and most people will conjure up images of grand residences, gardens and extensive country estates (not forgetting the ubiquitous gift shops and welcome tearooms). But looking after stately homes is only part of the Trust's remit. From its formation in 1931, its aims have included safeguarding Scotland's modest historic houses, then under threat from indiscriminate slum clearance. In 1932, Fife's medieval burgh of Culross became the first place to benefit from this enlightened policy, as the Trust began its programme of acquisition and preservation of the town's traditional buildings. The object was not to create museums, but to restore the townscape for the local community and provide, in the words of pioneering conservationist Ian Lindsay, 'civilised, decent homes of character and beauty'.

In 1960, in the face of a new wave of redevelopment, this flagship project became the model for the Trust's influential Little Houses Improvement Scheme, which introduced a revolving fund for buying up characterful traditional homes, undertaking their restoration and then reselling them. Beginning with two adjoining 17th-century houses in Crail, the initial activity of the scheme again focused largely on Fife, and by 1975 it had paid for the restoration of around 140 historic dwellings in ancient towns including Dysart (upper photo) and St Monans (lower photo).

Two of the most charming characteristics of these vernacular houses are their distinctive crow-stepped gables and pantiled roofs. The wavy clay rooftiles were at first imported from Holland, until enterprising architect William Adam set up a Scottish pantile works at Linktown, Kirkcaldy in 1714. The stairstep style of gable evolved due to the difficulty of cutting sandstone on a diagonal, with the bonus of facilitating access for roof repairs and chimney cleaning – a neat and stylish marriage of form and function.

Address Photo 1: Hie-Gait, Dysart, KY1 2UR; Photo 2: 4–5 & 6 Mid Shore, St Monans, KY10 2BA | **Getting there** 1: bus 7, 7A, X60 or X61 to Dysart (Porte); 2: bus 95 or X60 to St Monans (Station Road) | **Tip** In addition to the little houses in Culross, Crail, Dysart and St Monans, dozens of others restored under the Improvement Scheme can be found in Pittenweem, Anstruther, Cellardyke, Elie, Arncroach, Kingsbarns, Falkland, Newburgh, Tayport and Kincardine. They are identifiable by discreet plaques featuring variants of the National Trust for Scotland's logo of a saltire and castle.

110 The Pilgrim Way

Take the road less travelled

In the Middle Ages, pilgrimage was a physical journey towards a spiritual goal: to fulfil a vow, seek a miraculous cure, expiate wrongdoing or just ensure salvation. The earliest Christian pilgrims visited the land where Jesus and his followers had lived; in later centuries, however, as the physical evidence of saints' existence became scattered throughout Christendom, the pious began to travel in large numbers to the shrines of Europe that held the most venerated remains.

As the home of the bones of Christ's first disciple, St Andrews was in the top three destinations for spiritual tourism (after Rome and Compostela), and for 400 years before the Reformation brought a violent end to relic-worship, pilgrims poured into Fife from far and near. Their journeys might have involved fun and adventure, but they were also slow, arduous and often dangerous, and a vast infrastructure of roads, ferries, bridges, chapels, hospitals and inns was established to help travellers on their way.

One well-trodden route has been recreated as the Fife Pilgrim Way, a 64-mile trail starting from either Culross or North Queensferry. Waymarkers with a logo based on a 15th-century pilgrim's badge guide you through its eight stages. You can take in atmospheric landmarks such as Inverkeithing Hospitium, the healing well of St Finglassin and the superb Norman tower of St Drostan's, Markinch; there are many stretches where you're alone with the beauties of nature, and the route has also been designed to incorporate terrain related to Fife's mining heritage. Towards the end you proceed up the Waterless Road to Ceres before crossing the Bishop's Bridge, where the final section begins. Scottish pilgrims were famed throughout Europe for walking with their shoes tied round their necks; that is not recommended today, although the paths are well made, mostly level, and considerably easier to negotiate than the uneven and often boggy tracks that medieval travellers had to contend with.

Address From Culross or North Queensferry to St Andrews; the photo shows Bishop's Bridge, Ceres. See www.fifecoastandcountrysidetrust.co.uk for full details and maps; route data can be downloaded to your phone. | **Getting there** Train to North Queensferry; bus to Culross; good public transport links along the way | **Tip** The other main route to St Andrews was by boat from North Berwick to Earlsferry (now merged with Elie). The remains of a hostel, where pilgrims stayed before continuing overland, can be seen on Chapel Green. In the year 1413 alone, the ferry service was used by 15,000 people.

111 Waymarkers and Milestones

Show me the way to go home

The die-cut, retro-reflective signage that guides today's motorists round the highways of Scotland may be admirably clear, but it's sadly lacking in character compared with the traditional aids to travellers that once lined its roads. Fife has a particularly rich heritage of 19th-century milestones, waymarkers and guide plates, and exemplary efforts have been made to preserve and document the 170-odd that survive: few counties have so many of different types, still on their original sites. During World War II, local authorities were instructed to remove or deface all signs that could be of use to the enemy; most were never put back, but a conscientious council surveyor ensured that Fife's were carefully stored, and they were reinstated in 1950.

In the late 18th century a new highway system began to take shape across the Kingdom, funded by tolls levied at turnpike barriers. Milestones were required to be placed at intervals along the turnpike roads, with wayside markers at junctions. The trusts who maintained the roads adopted a variety of distinctive designs for these, though all were made from whinstone and/or cast iron, and painted white with the information picked out in black. Many milestones were also incised with benchmarks, used to calculate altitude.

Not only do they mark the distances, often down to fractions of a mile, they also provide a historical record of forgotten ferry ports and lost staging posts, although the abbreviated place names may puzzle non-Fifers. Several even let you know when you've arrived, such as the cast-iron sign on the old Great Fife Road whose list of places ends 'Newport 0'. There are many local fans of these unique monuments who are committed to ensuring their survival: the charming guide post at Arncroach (photo 1) is in fact a faithful replica, erected recently after the original was stolen.

	MILES		MILES
GIBLISTON	1½	LOCHTY	2½
LATHALLAN	3½	HIGHAM	4
LARGOWARD	4½	PEAT INN	5½
GILSTON	5½	CUPAR	12
MONTRAVE	10	ST ANDREWS	9½

Address Photo 1: B 9171, 0.1 mile north of Arncroach; photo 2: Lower Largo, on A 915 at the junction with Harbour Wynd. The majority of the best preserved are in the East Neuk; many are marked on Ordnance Survey maps. For a comprehensive list, see *The Milestones of Fife* by Alex Darwood and Paula Martin | **Getting there** Car, bus or on foot | **Tip** Just north of Kinghorn, on the back road that links the B 923 and the B 1957, look out for the Kissing Trees: two mature sycamores, directly opposite each other, that meet high above the road in what appears to be a tender embrace.

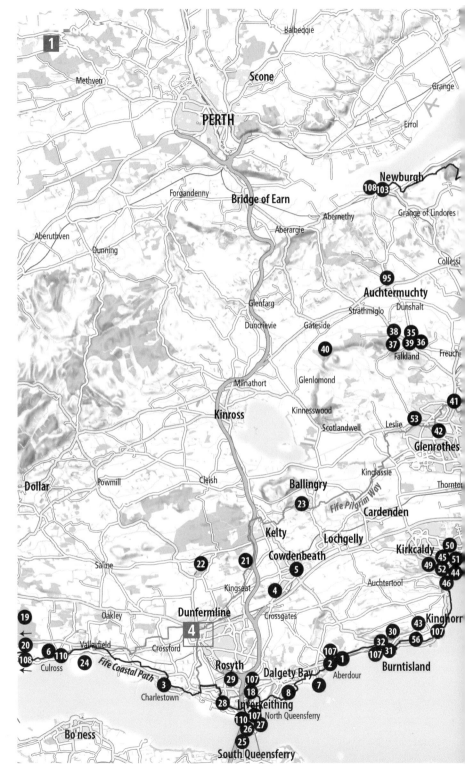

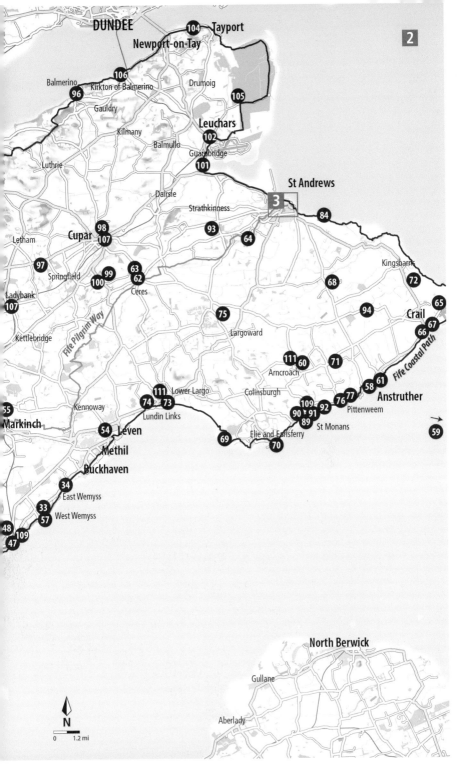

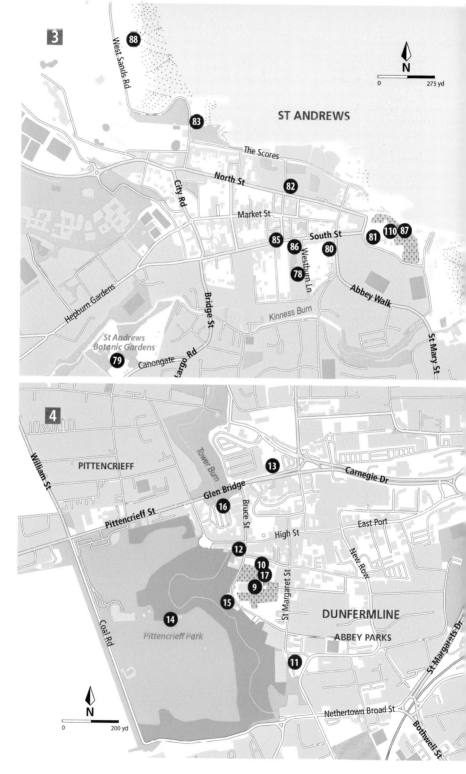

Gillian Tait
111 Places in Edinburgh
That You Shouldn't Miss
ISBN 978-3-96041-156-7

Tom Shields, Gillian Tait
111 Places in Glasgow
That You Shouldn't Miss
ISBN 978-3-7408-1488-5

Elizabeth Atkin, Laura Atkin
111 Places in County Durham
That You Shouldn't Miss
ISBN 978-3-7408-1426-7

David Taylor
111 Places along Hadrian's Wall
That You Shouldn't Miss
ISBN 978-3-7408-1425-0

Ed Glinert, David Taylor
111 Places in Yorkshire
That You Shouldn't Miss
ISBN 978-3-7408-1167-9

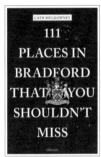

Cath Muldowney
111 Places in Bradford
That You Shouldn't Miss
ISBN 978-3-7408-1427-4

Kim Revill, Alesh Compton
111 Places in Leeds
That You Shouldn't Miss
ISBN 978-3-7408-0754-2

Michael Glover,
Richard Anderson
111 Places in Sheffield
That You Shouldn't Miss
ISBN 978-3-7408-1728-2

Julian Treuherz,
Peter de Figueiredo
111 Places in Manchester
That You Shouldn't Miss
ISBN 978-3-7408-0753-5

Julian Treuherz,
Peter de Figueiredo
111 Places in Liverpool
That You Shouldn't Miss
ISBN 978-3-7408-1607-0

David Taylor
111 Places in Newcastle
That You Shouldn't Miss
ISBN 978-3-7408-1043-6

Katherine Bebo, Oliver Smith
111 Places in Poole
That You Shouldn't Miss
ISBN 978-3-7408-0598-2

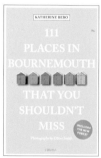

Katherine Bebo, Oliver Smith
111 Places in Bournemouth
That You Shouldn't Miss
ISBN 978-3-7408-1166-2

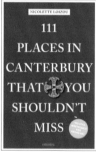

Nicolette Loizou
111 Places in Canterbury
That You Shouldn't Miss
ISBN 978-3-7408-0899-0

Philip R. Stone
111 Dark Places in England
That You Shouldn't Miss
ISBN 978-3-7408-0900-3

John Sykes, Birgit Weber
111 Places in London
That You Shouldn't Miss
ISBN 978-3-7408-1168-6

Ed Glinert, Marc Zakian
111 Places in London's East End
That You Shouldn't Miss
ISBN 978-3-7408-0752-8

Solange Berchemin,
Martin Dunford, Karin Tearle
111 Places in Greenwich
That You Shouldn't Miss
ISBN 978-3-7408-1107-5

Nicola Perry, Daniel Reiter
33 Walks in London
That You Shouldn't Miss
ISBN 978-3-95451-886-9

Kirstin von Glasow
111 Gardens in London
That You Shouldn't Miss
ISBN 978-3-7408-0143-4

Laura Richards, Jamie Newson
111 London Pubs and Bars
That You Shouldn't Miss
ISBN 978-3-7408-0893-8

Emma Rose Barber, Benedict Flett
111 Churches in London
That You Shouldn't Miss
ISBN 978-3-7408-0901-0

Solange Berchemin
111 Places in the Lake District
That You Shouldn't Miss
ISBN 978-3-7408-0378-0

Rob Ganley, Ian Williams
111 Places in Coventry
That You Shouldn't Miss
ISBN 978-3-7408-1044-3

Martin Booth, Barbara Evripidou
111 Places in Bristol
That You Shouldn't Miss
ISBN 978-3-7408-1612-4

Alexandra Loske
111 Places in Brighton and
Lewes That You Shouldn't Miss
ISBN 978-3-7408-1727-5

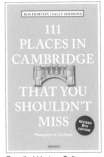

Rosalind Horton, Sally
Simmons, Guy Snape
111 Places in Cambridge
That You Shouldn't Miss
ISBN 978-3-7408-1285-0

Justin Postlethwaite
111 Places in Bath
That You Shouldn't Miss
ISBN 978-3-7408-0146-5

Kai Oidtmann
111 Places in Iceland
That You Shouldn't Miss
ISBN 978-3-7408-0030-7

Andrea Livnat,
Angelika Baumgartner
111 Places in Tel Aviv
That You Shouldn't Miss
ISBN 978-3-7408-0263-9

Sybil Canac, Renée Grimaud,
Katia Thomas
111 Places in Paris
That You Shouldn't Miss
ISBN 978-3-7408-0159-5

Thomas Fuchs
111 Places in Amsterdam
That You Shouldn't Miss
ISBN 978-3-7408-0023-9

Rüdiger Liedtke
111 Places in Mallorca
That You Shouldn't Miss
ISBN : 978-3-7408-1049-8

Alexia Amvrazi,
Diana Farr Louis, Diane Shugart,
Yannis Varouhakis
111 Places in Athens
That You Shouldn't Miss
ISBN 978-3-7408-0377-3

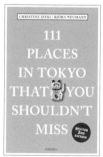

Christine Izeki, Björn Neumann
111 Places in Tokyo
That You Shouldn't Miss
ISBN 978-3-7408-1277-5

Christoph Hein, Sabine Hein
111 Places in Singapore
That You Shouldn't Miss
ISBN 978-3-7408-0382-7

Many friends have helped me with this book in a variety of funda-mental respects, by generously providing accommodation, transport and useful literature, as well as with considered suggestions and advice. I would particularly like to express my heartfelt gratitude to Rosa Steppanova, James Mackenzie, Judith Anderson, Mike Wragg, Maureen Grimshaw, Christine Bullick, Anne Bunyan, Henry Noltie, Susan Ross, Liz Thomson, Anne Jones, Fiona Allardyce, Ben Thurman, Tom Hubbard, Malcolm Crosby and Richard Brewster. I would also like to thank the following for their kind assistance with photography and research during the time I spent visiting their 'places': Lis McTaggart (ch. 2), Garry Irvine (ch. 26), Jim McLaughlin (ch. 32), Fiona Wemyss (ch. 33), Ewan Lee (ch. 35), Bob Beveridge (ch. 39), Tom Moffet (ch. 57), Griselda Hill and Elaine Syme (ch. 63), Sarah Johnson and Largo (ch. 75), Bob Robertson and Peter Adamson (ch. 79), Ross Wilson (ch. 99), Paul Dodman and Marije de Vries (ch. 103), and Lynette Gray (ch. 107).

In the course of my travels I met many knowledgeable individuals who contributed to my research in all sorts of ways; they are, sadly, too numerous to mention, but I especially want to record my thanks to Bruce Manson of Markinch, Ian Archibald of Burntisland, the gentle fossil hunter Sam McAuliffe, the friendly receptionist (and proud descendant of Queen Margaret) at Dunfermline City Chambers, and the solicitous walker I met at Kinkell Ness on 22 July, 2019, who saved me from dehydration on a hot day.

Edinburgh Central Library's Scottish Collection was a fantastic resource for me throughout this project, as was the excellent Fife Weather website operated by Graham Smith. Finally, I must mention the key role played by the feline and canine friends I made during the weeks that I spent pet-sitting at their homes in the Kingdom, who helped me immeasurably just by being their inimitable selves: Pepper of Burntisland, Seth and Sasha of Strathkinness, Ollie, Bailey and Jasper of Freuchie, and Sam, Hedwig and Newton of Kirkcaldy.

Gillian Tait was born in Edinburgh, and grew up in other parts of Scotland. She studied art history and painting conservation at the universities of Edinburgh and London respectively, and worked for many years in the museum sector in Scotland, England and the USA. In more recent years she has occupied her time as a writer, editor and photographer, while indulging her passions for travel, singing and performing in opera, operetta and musical theatre, and improving her Italian. Her first book in this series, as author and photographer, was *111 Places in Edinburgh that you Shouldn't Miss,* and she subsequently contributed to *111 Places in Glasgow that you Shouldn't Miss* as both photographer and editor. She lives in the heart of Edinburgh's Old Town.